Social unrest and popular protest in England 1780–1840

Prepared for the Economic History Society by

John E. Archer
Edge Hill College of Higher Education, Ormskirk

CAMBRIDGE
UNIVERSITY PRESS

PUBLISHED BY THE PRESS SYNDICATE OF THE UNIVERSITY OF CAMBRIDGE
The Pitt Building, Trumpington Street, Cambridge, United Kingdom

CAMBRIDGE UNIVERSITY PRESS
The Edinburgh Building, Cambridge CB2 2RU, UK   www.cup.cam.ac.uk
40 West 20th Street, New York, NY10011-4211, USA   www.cup.org
10 Stamford Road, Oakleigh, Melbourne 3166, Australia
Ruiz de Alarcón 13, 28014 Madrid, Spain

First published 2000

Printed in the United Kingdom at the University Press, Cambridge

Typeset in Plantin 10/12.5 pt [VN]

A catalogue record for this book is available from the British Library

Library of Congress cataloguing in publication data
Archer, John E.
Social unrest and popular protest in England, 1780–1840/John E. Archer.
    p.   cm. – (New studies in economic and social history)
Includes bibliographical references and index.
ISBN 0 521 57216 9
1. England – Social conditions – 18th century.   2. England – Social conditions –
19th century.   3. Demonstrations – England – History.   4. Social conflict –
England – History.   5. England – Economic conditions – 18th century.
6. England – Economic conditions – 19th century.   I. Title.   II. Series.
HN398.E5 A73 2000
306'.0942'09033 – dc21   00-028955

ISBN 0 521 57216 9 hardback
ISBN 0 521 57656 3 paperback

Contents

JAN 2 6 2001

Preface

In the years between 1780 and 1840 England experienced considerable change and tensions associated with the so-called Industrial Revolution, urbanisation, population growth and a long-term war with France that lasted for a generation. This book is concerned both with the disturbances and protests generated by these changes and with the debates between social historians who have studied this period. A number of parameters have been imposed on this study: namely, the coverage is restricted to England, and it ends when Chartism makes its appearance in the late 1830s.

1
Introduction: historiography, sources and methods

The study of popular protest and social unrest has burgeoned since the 1960s. Before then only a handful of historians had shown any inclination either for rescuing the masses as historical actors in their own right, or for allowing acts of protest any historical significance or importance. 'High politics' with the mob playing a subsidiary walk-on role had, until then, dominated historical writing. There were exceptions, such as the Hammonds (1920), Darvall (1936) and Wearmouth (1945). Their work, however, failed to establish the sub-genre of social history which the study of protest was to become. The belief that protest in the form of riots and social movements has much to tell us of society, particularly of the masses who normally left little historical record, was championed by a triumvirate of British marxist social historians: George Rudé, E. P. Thompson and Eric Hobsbawm. Possessing the same motivation for writing 'history from below' and rescuing, in the now-famous phrase of Thompson, 'the poor stockinger, the Luddite cropper, the "obsolete" hand-loom weaver, the "utopian" artisan, and even the deluded follower of Joanna Southcott, from the enormous condescension of posterity' (1968: 13), these three historians made distinctive but complementary contributions to our understanding of popular protest. In the process they generated a continuing interest from a new generation of researchers and scholars.

Rudé has been credited with identifying the 'faces in the crowd', as has Hobsbawm for the phrase and the concept of 'bargaining by riot', whilst Thompson is remembered both for his 'making of the working class' thesis and for the influential 'moral economy' concept, which was originally attached to food rioting but has since been developed and deployed in the interpretation of many other protest gatherings. What these three, and subsequent historians, have been doing is trying to answer what appear to be simple questions: namely the 'who', 'what', 'when', 'where', 'why' and 'how' of protest. Such questions have produced answers which have led both to serious academic debate and disagreement, and to complex and sophisticated analysis and methodology. Consequently, historians now specialise in increasingly narrow fields of protest study. The one major exception is John Stevenson, whose work *Popular Disturbances in England 1700–1832* (1992) provides the fullest synthesis of protest in all its forms.

The question that primarily interested Rudé was who formed the mob. In fact, he suggested that the very terminology of 'mob', 'rabble', 'swinish multitude' (1964: 7–8) required greater critical examination because these descriptions were so resonant of contemporary elite prejudices and values. The negative connotations of mindless, ugly and anarchic violence, which many contemporaries associated with the 'mob', seemed inappropriate following closer historical research of riotous events such as the 1780 Gordon Riots. Rudé's pre-industrial urban crowd was, he found, composed not of the unemployed or the criminal sub-stratum, but of wage earners with rational beliefs and value systems who were in fact disciplined in their actions, in so far as they directed their anger at specific targets, and usually at property rather than people. Moreover, they were often attempting to re-establish the status quo, not to challenge it. Thompson, with his sophisticated 'moral economy' thesis, reinforced and added to this interpretation of the rational crowd by highlighting the ideology which motivated and activated protesters and which, by implication, accepted Hobsbawm's notion of the crowd bargaining with the authorities.

The crowd, or a collective gathering which riots or protests, is largely seen as the typical example of popular protest during this period. Recently Tilly has used the term 'contentious gathering' to describe much the same sort of phenomenon. The hijacking of the word 'crowd' as a methodological descriptor of a protest group has come under heavy criticism from Holton (1978) and Harrison (1988). The former argued that Rudé had failed to be exact or systematic enough in defining or conceptualising the notion of a crowd and that labour and social historians too narrowly regarded crowds solely as protesting crowds. In a similar vein Harrison has argued that people living in increasingly urbanising environments came together for a whole host of reasons: to celebrate or to spectate for example, as well as to protest. His was the first attempt, by a historian, to undertake a systematic study of 'mass phenomena' – his even more neutral term for crowds – in which the protesting or riotous crowd (which are not necessarily the same) are placed in the context of all forms of mass gatherings.

In many ways Harrison's most original and interesting contribution to the study of popular protest concerned the questions of at what time of the day and on what day of the week protest meetings took place. He discovered that three-quarters of Bristol's riotous crowds between 1790 and 1835 occurred outside working hours, either in the lunch break or in the evening, which implied that the participants were not the unemployed, but people in work who could not afford to take time off to form a riotous crowd during working hours (1988: 127). Moreover Monday, a non-working day for many (ibid.: 121–4), was the most frequent rioting day of the week. By way of emphasising the 'respectability' of the rioters Harrison has argued that the contemporary term 'rabble' specifically referred to the unemployed. Consequently, a riotous crowd which formed during working hours was perceived by the civic authorities to be more threatening than one organised in the evening when working people were able to attend.

The notion of a disciplined crowd even within a riot has been discussed and debated in the context of what Bohstedt has termed 'community' politics, class formation and conflict towards the end of the eighteenth century. He argued that popular mobilisation tended to be more violent and disorderly in industrial towns such as Manchester than in market towns in Devon, for example. This violence indicated, Bohstedt maintained, a breakdown in 'community' politics, social networks and local patronage (1983: 69–83). Riots were, in other words, more violent and threatening in the newly emerging towns and cities than in the older provincial centres. Industrialisation and urbanisation were disrupting traditional social relations and contributing to rising class conflict (ibid.: 99). Underpinning this debate is the issue of evolution and change in popular protest (Charlesworth 1993: 205–12). Was protest 'modernising' or 'progressing' towards more modern forms such as trade unions or political associations which were more organised, permanent and formal than the temporary, informal and mostly spontaneous riots of the eighteenth century?

The American historian Charles Tilly has spent thirty years tracing the changing features of British and European protest. Originally his highly teleological model identified 'reactive' or reactionary and defensive actions such as food rioting which evolved into more modern 'proactive' forms such as the trade union strike weapon (Tilly, Tilly and Tilly 1975: 250–1). Such an approach was implicitly endorsed in the model adopted by Geary (1981), who wrote of the development from pre-industrial to early industrial and finally modern labour protests. Both recognised the shortcomings of the evolutionary models, none more so than Tilly, who recently acknowledged the limitations of labels such as forward- and backward-looking protest (1995: 46–8). He has presented a more sophisticated model of change in 'contentious gatherings' between 1750 and the 1830s. These changes owed more to such impersonal forces as the growth of the state than to changes in popular culture. Whilst his approach is not wholly or solely 'history from below', he is clearly indebted to Thompson, Rule and Wells, for example, who have related protest to the emergence of a working class. In so doing they have viewed the 1790s as a crucial decade when the 'consumerist mentality' of food rioters gave way to democratic political and proletarian demands and principles (Wells 1988: 74–5). Although this decade has been identified as something of a watershed, most historians tend to emphasise the lack of a clean break in protest methods between the middle of the eighteenth and the early nineteenth centuries. Elements of continuity in industrial protest, for example, are discernible and, more importantly, so is the propensity of rioters to utilise different methods of protest during disputes. Nowhere is this more evident than in the industrialising North, where food riots, industrial strife and secret political associations were so intermixed as to make it impossible to separate the various protest strands. Debate has arisen, for example, over Luddism, between Thomis and Thompson to name but two protagonists; the point at issue is the former's separation of the phenomenon of Luddism from underlying radical and conspiratorial manifestations of social and political unrest. The general consensus appears to favour those who put forward a more sophisticated and multifaceted picture of popular unrest that includes a community as well as a class analysis. In a critique of Thompson, Colhoun (1982) jettisoned the class-based model of Luddism for one reliant on defensive community traditionalism.

The question as to where protest occurred has attracted new approaches, not least from the historical geographer Charlesworth, who has been able to provide several insights (1983, 1993; Charlesworth *et al.* 1996). By locating disturbances more precisely and placing them in their regional context, he has been able to identify strong communal and local solidarities during disputes. Even the most basic question, 'what', is still attracting new research that lies far beyond the limited confines of this short study. Riots over the price of tickets at Covent Garden Theatre in the early nineteenth century (Baer 1992) or against the Irish (Neal 1988) have, for example, been neglected by socialist-inclined historians who favoured the more politically attractive labour struggles, but these deserve to be viewed as manifestations of popular protest. A fuller account, which takes in a variety of grievances or 'manifold disorders', can be found in Stevenson (1992).

Sources, problems and methodologies

A wide range of sources has been examined by historians over the years. By far the most important and extensive are the varied official documents held in the Public Record Office. Most useful have been the Home Office (HO) Papers, particularly HO 40–45, which contain correspondence between the home secretary and local magistrates and other provincial dignitaries on disturbances in their locales. Further provincial correspondence on riots can be found under HO 52 and, where trials arose, the Treasury Solicitor's Papers occasionally add details to those in the Assize Papers.

County record offices can hold a wealth of valuable material, not least the Quarter Sessions and local yeomanry records, and the correspondence of Lord Lieutenants, who were the county leaders responsible for upholding law and order and liaising with government. In recent years, the most popular source for scholars has been the local press, usually weekly newspapers, which provide a fund of detail on riots, incendiary fires and trials arising out of popular disturbances. For major outbreaks of trouble, the national daily press, such as *The Times*, carried reports. One biweekly usefully mined by E. P. Thompson (1975a) was *The Weekly Gazette*, which published transcriptions of threatening and anonymous letters carrying government rewards. These letters offer historians an insight into the thoughts of those who rarely left any other historical trace, whilst memoirs by radicals like Samuel Bamford offer authentic eyewitness accounts relating to political protest which counterbalance the official view, as indeed does the radical press of which Cobbett's *Political Register* is the most famous. Students with access to the internet will find web sites such as www.spartacus.schoolnet.co.uk useful, as this provides documentary extracts relating, for example, to Luddism and Peterloo.

The most important drawback to local and national records is their provenance. They largely represent the views of authority. Whilst historians are aware of this bias and can take it into account, they cannot always gauge the accuracy of such reports, particularly those which attempted to estimate numbers involved in demonstrations and riots. Likewise, the veracity of some records has to be questioned if the author was a government spy. A further problem arises from the possible exaggeration contained in letters to the Home Office from nervous magistrates who could, on occasion, exaggerate the scale of the disorder in their attempt to have troops deployed to their area. The biggest and most insurmountable problem relates to the 'dark figure', that is those popular disturbances which were unreported and have left no literary trace. Occasionally, historians discern hints in press reports of events having taken place but, because of their relative insignificance or the fear that their reports might lead to 'copy-cat' riots elsewhere, newspapers failed to divulge further details.

This lack of definitive and comprehensive information can have important and damaging repercussions for those historians who employ a quantifying methodology. This is especially applicable to the American school of Bohstedt, Munger and Tilly, who appear more willing than their British counterparts to use computers in creating their datasets. For Bohstedt (1983), a riot constituted 50 or more persons, and for Tilly (1995: appendix 1) just ten or more qualified as a contentious gathering. One immediate problem in adopting this kind of approach lies in the fact that press and official reports were never detailed enough to allow for such exact numbers. More importantly, by defining popular disturbances and contentions as involving a group of people – Stevenson, for example, has argued that the defining characteristics of popular disturbances are 'numbers and violence' (1992: 12) – these historians are neglecting individual acts of protest such as arson and animal maiming, which arguably became the hallmark of rural protest from 1830. The most critical response to what might be termed the quantifying historians is that of Wells, who has emphasised the imprecision in this respect of the PRO records (1978: 68–72). The historian's judgement is crucial in assessing the veracity and accuracy of the source materials and in imposing an imaginative and empathetic but critical interpretation. It would be fair to conclude this chapter by observing that this branch of social history has, over the years, produced a host of very fine historians whose work this book now reviews.

2
Agricultural protest

The rural labouring communities of the Southern and Eastern counties of England not only entered the darkest decades of their history between the late eighteenth and the middle of the nineteenth centuries, they also suffered far more hardship and oppression than any other occupational group. Given the appalling state of rural England, the specific history of rural protest has not attracted, until recently, quite the same interest as have the Luddites or political reform. This is all the more surprising when it is remembered that rural Southern England was the arena both for the most widespread popular uprising of the nineteenth century – Captain Swing – and also for one of the bloodiest in the strange tale of Bosenden Wood. There have been two major exceptions to this neglect, first the Hammonds' study of 1911 (1920) and the more influential work on *Captain Swing* by Hobsbawm and Rudé (1973). For many years it was believed that, with the exception of Swing and Tolpuddle, there were few rural events worth investigating. This changed when the followers of E. P. Thompson, and of Hobsbawm and Rudé, armed with doctorates covering most grain-growing counties of Southern and Eastern England, set about destroying the English rural idyll so resonant in earlier histories. Figuratively speaking, the 'ploughs and cows' economically oriented histories (the phrase is Snell's), were smashed or maimed by this younger generation of historians.

There is, however, a large measure of agreement on the condition of the farm labourers who, during the course of the eighteenth century, experienced a progressive deterioration in terms of both their standard of living and their quality of life (Reed and Wells 1990: 29-53). Three words would seem to describe the downward spiral into which they were sucked: proletarianisation, pauperisation and disinheritance. Such alterations were both the cause and the consequence of wider social and economic structural changes. These changes affected all social groups, including the ruling gentry and farmers, whose attitudes towards the poor increasingly included the rejection of the paternalistic code of previous centuries in favour of market and individualistic values. There was, in effect, a transformation in social relations which most historians locate as having occurred by the period of the Napoleonic wars.

Farm labour, particularly in East Anglia, was progressively switching from live-in farm service, in which labourers shared the same table and slept under the same roof as their masters, to casual weekly and day labour. The demographic pressures of enormous population growth, combined with the huge rise in food prices, especially wheat, between the 1790s and 1815, meant that employers found it more economical and socially attractive to make this switch. Younger labourers for the most part welcomed the move, since many found life in the farmhouse irksome and constricting. A number of effects resulted from this change, not least the lowering of the age of marriage which fed further population growth and, in time, a growing pool of under- and unemployed labour (Snell 1987: 67–103). The seasonality of arable agriculture meant that farmers could draw on an increasing body of labour in the peak months and then lay them off in winter. This was especially true in the years after the Napoleonic wars when over a quarter of a million labourers were demobilised. Unemployment and underemployment had, by the time of the 1830 Swing Riots, become permanent features of arable England, which was then experiencing some of the darkest years of the century.

Wages followed a similar downward spiral. In 1780, East Anglia was one of the highest wage regions in the country but had, by the 1830s, slipped to being the lowest. Only the Northern and industrialising regions kept up relatively high wages because of the alternative employment opportunities available to rural communities. Moreover, with the progressive casualisation of day labouring and the huge rise in prices between 1780 and 1815, farmworkers could no longer command 'just' or living wages. T. L. Richardson (1993), in his study of Lincolnshire, has shown that wages failed to keep pace with the volatile movement in prices, particularly wheat, and that this had a dreadful impact on the standard of living of farmworkers.

Traditional mechanisms for linking wages to the cost of wheat were simply jettisoned by farmers, who responded to the market forces of supply and demand. Labourers found that they were no longer 'worthy of their hire'. This becomes especially evident when the farmers' manipulation of the Poor Law is examined. The Speenhamland system of 1795, which was devised to meet the short-term emergency of high food prices, was a paternalistic attempt to stop labouring families from starving by tying the amount of relief to the price of bread and the size of their families. However, in time this and more stringent variants, such as the roundsman system, were utilised by farmers to push down wages to absolute minima in the full knowledge that other non-employing ratepayers would have to subsidise the wages of their workforce (Snell 1987: 104–14).

The labourer and his family were, as a result, reduced to the status of paupers, with all the connotations of idleness, immorality and depravity attached to that label. For the labourer's part, notions of self-respect and dignity could be kept up only through displays of deference on the one hand or through acts of protest on the other. It would be erroneous to assume that the former mode of behaviour was anything other than a role acted out by the poor, who in many circumstances came to realise that charity and relief were dependent upon externalised patterns of behaviour. This explains to a great extent the shocked surprise often expressed by ruling elites whenever major outbursts of rustic anger occurred. They had simply misread deferential behaviour for deferential attitudes.

Enclosures and lost rights

Much controversy and debate have surrounded the poor's disinheritance from the land and from traditional customary rights such as gleaning, wood collecting, commoning and village festivities. The Hammonds (1920), more than anyone else, set out the thesis that enclosure was of central importance to rural protest. The core of their argument laid stress on the disappearance of the eighteenth-century peasantry who in turn became a disinherited landless proletariat. Over six million acres, or a quarter of the country's cultivated area, were enclosed under parliamentary acts between 1750 and 1850, the majority of both the acts and the enclosures occurring in the war years from 1793 to 1815. This proved devastating to small farmers, cottagers and squatters (ibid.: 73) who no longer had access to land. This 'class robbery' (E. P. Thompson 1968: 237) led to despair and fatalism. Later generations of economic historians have – vainly, as it has turned out – tried to redress this bleak interpretation. The process of enclosure was, for Chambers and Mingay (1966: 77–105), not only as fair and equitable as it could be for the period, but more importantly it also made English agriculture more efficient and productive. Whilst they concede that cottagers were proletarianised, they see this as a small social price worth paying. Furthermore, when the 1830 riots broke out in the Southern and Eastern counties, these areas had largely been enclosed for centuries. The newly enclosed Midland counties were generally quiescent. Both sides in this debate accepted the traditional view that enclosure rarely sparked off resistance at the time that it was actually taking place, although E. P. Thompson warned against overstating the apparent passivity of the victims until more research had been completed (1968: 240). Snell (1987: 138–227), and more recently Neeson (1993), have surely destroyed the economic historians' view with irrefutable evidence of the destruction of the land and common rights of smallholders and commoners and of their ways of life. Most importantly in this context, Neeson shows clearly that in Northamptonshire the 'peasantry' did not accept these changes passively, which may suggest that other well-documented enclosure disturbances, such as that at Otmoor (Reaney 1970), may be the rule rather than the exception. Opposition through courts of law was often futile and expensive; likewise riot and petitions met with little success (Neeson 1993: 263), but Neeson's work has revealed evidence of long wars which included the sending of threatening letters, the destruction of property and damage to fencing, hedges and gates (ibid.: 279, Eastwood 1996). Although riots marked the collective and most visible highpoint of these communal disturbances, the individual acts of sabotage, such as arson, were the most enduring. This was certainly the case in the parish of Ashill, Norfolk, where the author of an anonymous letter clearly had not forgotten or forgiven the 'jentlemen' for the 1785 enclosure (Neeson 1993: 256). The Napoleonic wars, it would seem, had delayed the full impact and implications of enclosure until 1816 when escalating poor rates and massive unemployment afflicted the village.

Unless protest occurred at the actual time of enclosure, itself a lengthy business, how then were Hobsbawm and Rudé, or the Hammonds, able to link the two? For the Hammonds and Neeson, who accepted the existence of a substantial eighteenth-century peasantry, enclosure destroyed a way of life for many, stripping the commoners of their independence and 'mutuality' and transforming them into a rural working class. The redefining of property ownership under capitalism left the dispossessed with feelings of injustice and anger which entered the 'folk memory'. This may have created a long-standing tradition of class warfare in later years (Neeson 1993: 292, 330). Not all historians of the left would agree with this interpretation. Hobsbawm and Rudé have emphasised the existence of the tripartite social structure of landlord, tenant farmer and labourer by 1750 (1973: 6; Reed and Wells 1990: 29–53). Enclosure, for them, was just one of many forces (and not the most important) speeding up the process of proletarianisation. Recently enclosed parishes tended to become locales of high poor rates, under- and unemployment, and consequently were troublesome in 1830. The debate has been complicated by the fact that the English peasant has been rediscovered skulking in nineteenth-century Sussex and Kent (Reed 1984) and any definitive conclusion on this theme may turn on definitions as much as anything else, for one historian's peasant is another's small farmer. However, there is no denying the fact that a substantial group lost rights.

This sense of disinheritance was compounded by changes in statute law which criminalized previously legitimate activities. It is within this arena that we find the most explicit clashes between plebeian and official cultures, that continued well into the nineteenth century. In some of the most stimulating research, the roles and functions of customary behaviour and practice have been rescued (Bushaway 1982a; E. P. Thompson 1991). This has been no easy task, as such traditions are rarely documented and by definition customs were usually legitimated by reference to regularly performed activities on an annual basis, or to 'time out of mind'. Only when the rural elites challenged these activities in the eighteenth century do historians gain an insight into their existence, functions and importance to the parochial poor. These customary activities were, however, increasingly viewed with dismay and distrust by the authorities, not least because they could become too rowdy and disorderly, and because they clashed with notions of property ownership as defined by statute law. Most significantly, where customary practices were still active, they gave the poor collective power. Defence of these traditions may be viewed as conservative and reactionary but, as E. P. Thompson noted, this rebelliousness was vital to the emerging class consciousness of the rural proletariat (1991: 8–13).

Wood gathering is a particularly interesting case in point. This centuries-old and nationwide practice was essentially criminalised in 1766 (Bushaway 1982a, and 1982b). The lack of cheap alternative sources of fuel for the poor meant that wood theft probably became the commonest crime in rural England, particularly during the French wars, when wood became such a valuable commodity and when enthusiasm for intensive game preserving was taking off. Wood theft as a survival or social crime (Rule 1979) and as a form of protest crime was often evident in parishes that had undergone enclosure, although it is hard to know where to draw the dividing line between protest in the form of 'hedge breaking' and the poor's need for fuel (Neeson 1993: 279–80). It is more than likely that hedge breaking and timber theft served this dual function in Chippenham, where a prosecuting association was established a year after enclosure. The protest content is much more explicit in the better-documented disputes at Great Wishford in Wiltshire and Otmoor in Oxfordshire. In the former, local landowner and game preserver, the Earl of Pembroke, attempted to halt the poor's right to wood, known as Grovely, but the women defended this right so successfully, in spite of some being gaoled, that the right continues to this day (Bushaway 1981: 43). In the case of Otmoor, under the guise of pursuing the traditional ritual of beating the bounds, 1,000 locals marched seven miles, destroying fences and hedges in the process. In this incident men reportedly dressed as women took a leading part in the destruction (Hammond and Hammond 1920: 64–72; Dunbabin 1974: 20). Cross dressing in English rural protest was, by this time, unusual and was never on the scale of Rebecca's Daughters in Wales in the 1840s (Jones 1989). Celebrations of saints' days could likewise allow the community to disguise their real intentions, St Andring's Day in Sussex being a case in point. Traditionally, the day allowed the people of the parish to go squirrel hunting, but anything that moved was shot and hedges were destroyed and carried home for fuel (Bushaway 1982a: 181).

With the exception of the Grovely dispute in Wiltshire, most attempts at keeping alive traditional rights were unsuccessful. Gleaning rights, which were universally practised throughout arable England, were perhaps the most notable exception. Unlike wood gathering, the gleaning of loose ears of corn by women and children after harvest was never criminalised, but in the famous Court of Common Pleas case of 1788 attempts were made by Essex farmers to prosecute women gleaners for trespass and theft. There were, the farmers argued, no legal sanctions which allowed gleaning and, as a result, they were successful in their prosecution for trespass. This led the Hammonds to assume that gleaning followed the way of other customary practices into extinction (1920: 84–5). More recent research has uncovered the uninterrupted practice of gleaning well into the nineteenth century and, more significantly, where court cases resulted from clashes between women gleaners and farmers, the former normally won in cases of assault (King 1989: 122–4). Conflicts arising out of clashes over customs and traditions could, and did, invite community anger of a highly ritualised character, such as rough music, effigy burning and 'skimmington'. In all three forms of demonstration, crowds set out to humiliate publicly anyone who had, in their opinion, broken community norms and unwritten rules, such as those against wife beating, adultery or informing on neighbours. In the case of rough music, crowds set up a cacophony of banging pots and pans outside the offender's house. 'Skimmington' and 'riding the stang' were regional terms for kinds of humiliating rituals which involved the victim, or someone representing the victim, riding a wooden horse or pole around the village while spectators shouted abuse at them. As a climax to community intimidation, the victim was occasionally burnt in effigy (E. P. Thompson 1991: 467–530).

Some crimes – poaching, smuggling and wood stealing, for example – have been categorised by historians as 'social crimes' because such activities were not viewed as being illegal by labouring communities in which the activities took place (Rule 1979). Poaching was a popularly sanctioned activity in which distinctions were drawn between wild birds and animals, pheasants and hares, which were the property of the person who found them, and farm animals, which were regarded as private property. From about the turn of the century, the clash between statute law and community attitudes fuelled an increasingly violent poaching war. 'The long affray', as

Hopkins (1985) termed it, developed into the most persistent and brutal campaign of nineteenth-century rural England (Jones 1982: 62). Whilst it would be wrong to regard this crime as a form of protest, since many 'poached for the pot' or for a living, poaching convictions certainly act as a useful index in determining the social and economic plight of farm labourers, as they had a tendency to rise shortly before years of protest (Muskett 1984: 4; Hobsbawm and Rudé 1973: 57). One should not, however, dismiss poaching as a protest crime because the Game Laws, and the manner in which game was preserved, were causes of considerable tension. As William Cobbett once observed, 'it is "nonsense to talk of peace and harmony in the country as long as that law should remain in existence"'(Hopkins 1985: 154).

Collective disturbances

Farmworkers rarely participated in food riots during this period. In the Eastern counties, however, they became involved in overt collective displays of protest once the Napoleonic wars ended. On the face of it, the cry of 'Bread or Blood', uttered in the Fenland towns and villages in 1816, suggests farmworkers were now involved in food rioting. Peacock's study (1965) is the first and only detailed examination of that year and it has largely stood the test of time. Important qualifications and refinements have since been added by Charlesworth (1983), who noted the involvement of textile workers and the presence of three types of riot. First, there was the food riot, in which agricultural labourers were hardly involved. The second and more significant type concerned attacks on threshing machines and mole ploughs used for drainage and, finally, there were angry demonstrations demanding higher wages. Charlesworth found the sheer variety of occupational groups involved in the disputes significant, and this fact may have contributed to the brutal repression that occurred in Downham and Littleport, both in Cambridgeshire, where protesters appear to have been unusually militant. In all, five were executed and most of the remaining seventy transported or imprisoned (ibid.: 146–7).

In 1822, with the return of agricultural depression, even more extensive rioting broke out in East Anglia, but this was further to the east towards the Norfolk–Suffolk border. Both Charlesworth (1983: 148–150) and Muskett (1984) have noted that these riots were basically hostile to threshing machinery and were the work of agricultural labourers. In terms of destruction, the 1822 riots were more concentrated and destructive than the 1830 Swing Riots in the region. Muskett has estimated that 52 machines were broken, yet very few of the 123 people arrested were transported. Many, in fact, received only short gaol sentences, and the only executions were of two Waterloo veterans who also fired property. The presence of war veterans led some magistrates to believe that some kind of conspiracy and organisation lay behind the riots (ibid.: 8; Archer 1990: 84). Whilst it has not been possible to explain why some parishes were more disturbed than others, it has been noted that the 1822 machine breaking represented an effective cull of machinery, since very few were destroyed here in 1830 (Muskett 1984: 11; Archer 1990: 90).

The climax to the mounting tensions brought about by agricultural depression and hard winters peaked in late August 1830 at Lower Hardres, Kent, when a threshing machine was destroyed. This event marked both the start of the Captain Swing Riots and announced its most distinctive feature, machine breaking (Hobsbawm and Rudé 1973: 71). There followed the most widespread bout of rural protest this country has ever experienced, with twenty-one English counties registering some kind of Swing activity in the remaining months of 1830, although isolated incidents of rural Luddism continued to occur into the summer of 1831 in Kent and East Anglia (Hobsbawm and Rudé 1973: 139).

What has so impressed historians is not simply the scale of Swing, its persistence or its variety of targets and protest weapons, but its many-layered complexities relating to social relations, and the political undertones which emerge here and there. The 'last labourers' revolt', as the Hammonds termed it, was far more widespread than they had documented, and with each succeeding generation of historians the scale appears ever greater. Thus Hobsbawm and Rudé's estimate of 1,475 incidents between 1830 and 1832 (1973: appendix 1) has been challenged by Wells and Archer, whose more focused local studies have recovered many more examples of machine breaking and arson. Even Swing's starting place and date have been disputed, with a claim for the expulsion of Irish harvesters from the Isle of Thanet in July as the first event (Reed and Wells 1990: 160). Whether this is a useful exercise is a moot point since attacks on Irishmen in Lincolnshire and the breaking of threshing machines had already begun in 1829 (T. L. Richardson 1993: 9; Archer 1990: 87–8).

Kent, however, was the recognised starting point, with the disturbances then spreading along and through the Southern counties of Surrey and Sussex (these three being the core counties), to Hampshire, Wiltshire and Dorset. Other arable regions were drawn in: the South Midland counties of Berkshire, Buckinghamshire and Oxford were all disturbed for two to three weeks in November. The East Anglian counties of Norfolk, Suffolk and Essex experienced a separate pattern of revolt, which was not altogether surprising given their history of machine breaking in 1816 and 1822 and their geographical isolation (Charlesworth 1979: 20).

Of the methods adopted by protesters, machine breaking was the most distinctive. However, arson arguably made its entrance as the labourers' primary weapon, and fire, it would seem, was the weapon feared most by farmers and the authorities, since its covert nature meant that it was hard to prevent, detect or eradicate. Moreover, it caused the greatest damage and consternation. In many counties fire acted both as a curtain raiser (especially in Norfolk where ten fires broke out a fortnight before the rioting), and as the final curtain when it became clear that the authorities were arresting and charging anyone who had the temerity to protest openly in broad daylight (Archer 1990: 90, 95). One other popular covert tactic during these months was the sending of threatening letters invariably signed by the ubiquitous Captain Swing. Authorities in a number of counties claimed to have caught the mythical Swing through his letter-writing activities. In Suffolk he was a primitive Methodist straw plait manufacturer distributing biblical threats; in Norfolk a radical weaver from Norwich; and, most famously, the self-styled 'Captain Hunt' in Hampshire, whose real name was James Cooper, an ostler from Wiltshire, who rode impressively around the countryside on a white horse, but was, sadly, mentally unhinged (Archer 1990: 94–5, 174; Hobsbawm and Rudé 1973: 93).

The public, open and often daylight displays of collective anger gave Swing its distinctive character. Rarely violent and often not riotous, but restrained and dignified in their anger, these mass mobilisations and demonstrations indicate that the variety of protest weapons reflected the wide range of grievances. In the Southern counties of Surrey and Sussex, Poor Law officials were unceremoniously bundled into parish poor carts and led to village boundaries. In most counties some forms of deputation were made with regard to low wages or Poor Law allowances, and in more extreme cases poorhouses were demolished, as at Selbourne in Hampshire. The assembled poor also left themselves open to prosecution for what the courts later defined as theft when they marched and paraded from one farm or parish to another, 'pressing' others into service and demanding levies of beer, food and money, or 'sturdy begging' as Cobbett termed it, from anyone who crossed their path (Hammond and Hammond 1920: 235).

Depending upon the central grievance or complaint, the Swing Riots threw up some surprising social alliances among the protesters. It would be simplistic and ahistorical to interpret these events purely in class terms, although it would be fair to observe that, where farmers encouraged their labourers to mob vicars and rectors for the reduction of tithes, they were attempting to deflect plebeian anger away from themselves on to an increasingly despised and remote group of churchmen (Evans 1976). This unlikely, if temporary, alliance was experienced in many counties and was concerned with a number of different issues. In south Norfolk and Sussex it was tithes. In many regions, smaller farmers were willing to see their own and their neighbours' machinery broken up, partly because threshing machines were no longer economical, but also because they were socially dangerous in so far as they created unemployment and raised the poor rates. Most importantly, their destruction prevented the large farmers from gaining an unfair advantage over the small farmer if all the machines in the neighbourhood were destroyed (Hobsbawm and Rudé 1973: 321–3). Thus, some of those in authority as employers, magistrates and landlords sided with the poor and the landless, and were ranged against their own class, which undermines those analyses which interpret the Swing movement solely in antagonistic class terms (Reed and Wells 1990: 162). Certainly, some farmers and justices of the peace were conciliatory for pragmatic reasons, buying time before reinforcements arrived; others acted opportunistically, as we have seen over the anti-tithe disturbances, but this does not explain the genuinely conciliatory and paternalistic responses the riots and demonstrations initially generated. In Wiltshire, where a quarter of all the threshing machines in England were broken, many of the gentry displayed genuine paternalistic concern for the labouring classes that probably went beyond expediency and fear of the mob (Randall and Newman 1995: 211–13). Magistrates advised farmers to raise wages or dismantle machinery, or passed derisory sentences on rioters. In Norfolk where the lord lieutenant ordered the discontinuance of machinery, thus lending a sense of legitimacy to the protesting labourers, the magistracy became divided between those in favour of customary social relations and those who supported the newer political economy (Hobsbawm and Rudé 1973: 123–5; Archer 1990: 91–2). Once the Whigs came into power in November 1830, attitudes at the Home Office hardened and magistrates were ordered to uphold the law strictly and not to interfere with the setting of wages or the use of machinery. Where labourers met with repression, resistance was at its fiercest. The behaviour of Benett, major landowner of the Pythouse estate, Wiltshire, who was adamant that no concessions should be granted to the demonstrators during the Tisbury riots, Wiltshire, shows how difficult it is to generalise about class relations, for the farmers sided with the labourers. His refusal to give way on the use of threshing machines led to his own being singled out for destruction, which, in turn, led to the killing of one of the rioters by the yeomanry (Hammond and Hammond 1920: 237–8; Randall and Newman 1995: 210–11).

The moderation of the Swing demonstrators (one hesitates to use the word rioters since many of the participants behaved peacefully and, as they thought, legitimately) suggests that they were behaving in time-honoured manner. The fact that the initial protesters were not heavily punished by magistrates suggests that they received a measure of sympathy and understanding from their social superiors. Physical violence was rarely resorted to by the rural populace, except in isolated incidents where the crowds met with resistance. The same cannot be said of the authorities, who in the harsh repression which followed sentenced 252 to death, of whom 19 were executed, and most of the reprieved transported to Australia (Rudé 1978).

Whilst the riots were widespread and all appear to have been repressed, the protests were in fact remarkably regionalised and localised. Large open parishes with a history of recent enclosure appear to have been more prone to Swing disturbances than smaller closed villages where paternal landlords were not only more likely to provide employment but also to control the activities of non-agricultural labourers, particularly skilled craftsmen like blacksmiths, carpenters and shoemakers who had reputations for radical politics (Reed and Wells 1990: 163). This partly explains the large number of non-agricultural workers arrested for machine breaking, but it also alerts us to the fact that machinery other than threshers was destroyed; sawmills and paper-making works, for example, both came under the hammer for making workers redundant.

One issue only recently addressed by historians concerns the geography or spatial diffusion of the riots. Originally, the spread of the disturbances was largely seen as haphazard and imitative – the 'copy-cat factor' in modern parlance – but it has taken the work of historical geographer, Charlesworth (1979, 1983), to move the analysis forward through his mapping of known incidents. His results display a strong correlation between the main London highways and the outbreak and subsequent spread of the riots, which suggest that the roads and those travelling on them, termed the 'link men' (1979: 37–9), were responsible for the transmission of news regarding the disturbances and, more intriguingly, that village craftsmen were kept in touch with the revolutions taking place on the continent, particularly France and Belgium, and the Reform Crisis then breaking in London. In this atmosphere of political turmoil, the riots take on a rather different complexion. The French tricolour; reportedly flying in a number of fairly remote parishes, lent the Swing Riots an insurrectionary character and suggest that readers of Cobbett's *Political Register* were busily mobilising the agrarian workforce who, in turn, through their display of collective strength and arson attacks, accelerated the movement for reform. This suggests that historians have seriously underestimated the political awareness of rural communities and have overemphasised the constricting character of the narrow and limited horizons of those living within these rural backwaters (Wells 1997). The farmworkers may well have been mobilised by radicals who had rather different agendas, but it is more than likely that the truly rural Swing episodes were motivated by loss and grievance which had their origins in the rural communities themselves, concerning issues such as work, wages, poor relief, the use of machinery and the role of rural elites. These factors concerned the majority of Swing's followers, but with the emergence of a political crisis, a European revolution and the prospect of another hard winter without work, the revolt became the most widespread on record, though it was not to be the last labourers' revolt.

Post-1830

The government established Special Commissions in Hampshire, Wiltshire, Dorset, Berkshire and Buckinghamshire to try the rioters. The home secretary did not entirely trust the local magistracy to be sufficiently harsh in serving out severe punishments to the guilty. The viciousness of the repression that followed led not to abject surrender but to a more deep-seated anger and a rural war which bordered on terrorism. Arson, animal maiming and even sheep stealing became enduring and covert forms of protest (Peacock 1974). The former was now made easier to commit and harder to detect with the invention and widespread availability of the strike-anywhere or 'lucifer' matches (Archer 1990: 73–4). Incendiarism especially became endemic after Swing and remained the hallmark of rural protest until well into the 1860s. In some cases it reached epidemic proportions, particularly in East Anglia, which has received most attention, but it also became predominant in counties which had largely been unaffected by the Swing Riots, such as Cambridgeshire, Devon and Yorkshire. This raises the question of whether covert individual protest replaced collective riots and demonstrations when the latter failed as a tactic and, if so, when? Such questions have been the source of considerable disagreement between Wells and Charlesworth, with the former robustly arguing that arson replaced collective actions in the 1790s. The latter's rebuttal that such a process began before the defeat of Swing has led to further refinements by Wells and others (Reed and Wells 1990). Although it is highly unlikely that arson replaced food rioting as a weapon of protest, since the former tended to occur with greater frequency at times of low rather than high wheat prices, it is undoubtedly true that individual covert social protest crime came to predominate by the mid- to late 1830s when issues relating to under- and unemployment, low wages and poor relief were the predominant worries affecting the rural poor.

But the dichotomy between overt and covert protest, so starkly delineated by the protagonists, may well be false for two important reasons. First, as has subsequently and repeatedly been demonstrated by historians, was the fact that covert and overt protest occurred simultaneously. One only has to think of the anti-New Poor Law disturbances of 1835 at Great Bircham, Norfolk, where farmers' homes were mobbed and, in one case, set alight (Peacock 1974: 37–8) or the anti-enclosure riots and fires at Otmoor, Oxfordshire (Eastwood 1996). Nor should we ignore the fact that threshing machines continued to be destroyed by pickaxe and sledgehammer, an altogether riskier and noisier proposition than burning, which became the favoured method of destruction after 1830. Second and more crucially, fire became the focal point of collective and perfectly legal – and some not so legal – displays of anger against the farming class. Crowds cheered as the flames consumed barns and crops, and many refused money and beer to fight the fires, whilst in the most extreme cases onlookers cut hoses, punctured buckets and even brought wood to toss on to the flames (Archer 1990: 157–61).

Whilst arson became the lasting and dominant method of protest, riot, demonstration and other collective actions did not fade away in the 1830s, which may suggest that some regions were more embittered than others. Nor had judicial repression and the supposed demise of paternalism prevented a few brief flirtations with trade unionism in Essex, Sussex and, more famously, Tolpuddle. Only with the introduction of the New Poor Law in 1835–6, the failure of the subsequent collective anger and the despair engendered do we see covert methods predominate. Changes in protest methods and tactics suggest that Swing failed, a point disputed by Wells and by Hobsbawm and Rudé. The spread of threshing machines was slowed and even halted for a number of years, wages and allowances were increased and, in some Southern counties, allotments were introduced. Many of these can be counted as temporary successes only, since evidence abounds, for example, that poor relief administration was progressively tightened with the introduction of professional relieving officers (Digby 1978: 47). This issue in itself led to a rise in anti-Poor Law protests prior to the Poor Law Amendment Act of 1834. Any protest movement which directly gave rise to a social welfare scheme of such unashamed harshness as the New

Poor Law cannot consider itself a success. The Swing Riots had given rise to the formation of a Royal Commission engaged in finding a solution to the Poor Law problem. The commission gathered evidence through *The Rural Queries*, a lengthy questionnaire, which inquired, among other things, as to whether communities had experienced trouble in 1830. Replies to this question have been usefully tabulated by Hobsbawm and Rudé (1973: 59).

Anti-New Poor Law protest

The Poor Law Amendment Act was passed in 1834 but began to be implemented, in piecemeal fashion, only from 1835. The most important provisions included in the act were the building of workhouses to serve the newly formed Poor Law unions which became administrative units. So far as the labouring poor were concerned, the able-bodied were no longer allowed outdoor relief as in former years; they had to receive relief in the workhouse. This institution was itself run along harsh lines, employing the principle of 'less eligibility' in order to make the life of the unemployed pauper less attractive than that of an independent labourer living in his own home (Digby 1978: 54–5). As a result, many of the rural poor felt they were being punished and stigmatized for their poverty. A sense of disinheritance emerges strongly from the embittered gatherings of men and women who came together to attempt both to halt the implementation of the New Poor Law in rural Southern and Eastern England and to defend outdoor relief and other allowances provided under the unreformed parochial system. Clear conceptions of 'rights', not least the right to receive cash payments from one's own community in times of distress, was evident both in the language the poor employed and in the modes of protest they adopted. Studies such as Digby (ibid.: ch. 1) that emphasise elements of continuity between the old and new Poor Laws fail to take on board the basic question: what did the recipients of these welfare reforms think? The reforms were perceived as being 'The Robbery Bill' (Rule and Wells 1997: 101), and the rural poor, the majority of whom would have at some time or other in their lives gone to the vestry for poor relief as a matter of course (Reay 1990: 78–9), feared that receipt of poor relief entailed imprisonment and the loss of liberty, the 'unchristian' separation of families into four categories defined by age and gender, as well as the stigma of pauperdom. Their humiliation, it would appear, was complete, as indeed was the destruction of the traditional community in which rich and poor subscribed to a common set of values and responsibilities (Knott 1986).

The anti-New Poor Law protests have been termed, with some justification, the 'last labourers' revolt' (Rule and Wells 1997: 125) because the demonstrations, fires and riots were widespread, if short-lived, in East Anglia, Bedfordshire and along the southern coast from Kent west to Cornwall. Although some studies (Edsall 1971; Knott 1986) underplay these rural disturbances in comparison with the Northern protests (see below: 73–4), it is more than likely that the full extent of anti-Poor Law feeling has yet to emerge (Randall and Newman 1995: 214). Patterns in the timing and the forms of protest are discernible and related very closely to the chronology of the implementation of the new legislation. Generally, protest was muted and quasi-legal petitions were raised initially, hardening to physical direct action against Poor Law guardians and relieving officers whose job it was to implement the new orders. Mass protests came at the final stage of the changeover when new workhouses were built and old ones extended. But the most persistent and enduring element in this drama was the long-term incendiarism experienced in many counties but most especially in the Eastern ones.

The first recorded instance of popular unrest, that of mobbing a relieving officer, came in April 1835 from the newly established Milton Union, Kent, where the method of paying allowances was altered from a cash payment to that of a ticket which the recipient exchanged for goods (Edsall 1971: 27–9). Neighbouring parishes were also upset at this ticket scheme, seeing it as unacceptable. The mobbing of relieving officers, particularly by women, rarely resulted in physical injuries to Poor Law officials, but it did cause many to fear for their physical safety and put their property at risk. At one of the very first anti-Poor Law disturbances in Norfolk, at Bircham in June 1835, the guardians (who were also farmers) foolishly reduced wages whilst simultaneously offering tickets in place of cash allowances to the needy. A crowd in excess of 800, according to local newspapers, 'bound in a bond of blood' marched to the overseer's house, stove in all the windows and doors and piled up the furniture, which they set alight before marching off into the night to another overseer's home (Knott 1986: 68–70; Digby 1978: 221–2). Such riots died away as quickly as they had flared up and by the time the army arrived the neighbourhood had become peaceful.

The next phase was more prolonged and better documented since it related to the establishment of the dreaded workhouses or 'bastilles'. The imposition of new orders relating to the workhouse test, the separation of families and the pauper diets provided the ingredients that had the potential to spark off riots as widespread and as dangerous as Swing. Sussex once again experienced one of the early flare-ups, when the Horsham guardians decided to use different poorhouses for different categories of paupers. The presence of an angry crowd forced the authorities to move the paupers to their respective institutions by armed guard at night (Rule and Wells 1997: 99). The following Christmas many local authorities in East Suffolk, where tensions had been building through the summer, came close to losing control. The Poor Law assistant commissioner, Kay, even had himself sworn in as a special constable after being assaulted during his travels around the county. First, Ipswich rose when the townspeople began to demolish one of the workhouses, and a further five were attacked in neighbouring unions by farm labourers armed with pickaxes and by inmates. At Semer the latter reduced the building to a 'state of incipient demolition' and defecated on the floors of their wards in a manner which presaged the 'dirty' protests in Northern Ireland in the late 1970s, when members of the Provisional IRA protested against their ordinary criminal status in the Maze prison (Archer 1990: 104). The army and the metropolitan police were for a number of weeks stretched almost to breaking point, and even where the workhouses were not yet built, as at Depwade, Norfolk, soldiers had to guard builders who initially had to construct pill boxes and the outer perimeter wall before turning to the actual building (Knott 1986: 81).

These collective disturbances in the South East, East Anglia and even Devon declined dramatically in 1836 after the firm response from the authorities had driven protest 'underground'. The riots had never been able to take off in the same way as Swing because the implementation of the reforms had been staggered in the different counties and unions. Moreover, the poor were never able to attract the support of their social and wealthier superiors to any great extent since the latter quickly appreciated the savings on the poor rates that the reforms were already accruing. Protest thereafter tended to be spontaneous, flaring up whenever Poor Law regulations were altered. It is debatable, however, whether this protest moderated the worst excesses of Poor Law practice in later years, although Wells has argued that covert responses after 1836, often in the form of arson, animal maiming and the sending of threatening and anonymous letters, were partly successful in ensuring that outdoor relief for married men continued (Reed and Wells 1990: 170).

Whilst arson was frequently resorted to after 1836, the New Poor Law gave rise to one of the strangest episodes on record. The Battle of Bosenden Wood of 1838 in which twenty people lay dead, dying or injured has been described as being definitively 'the last labourers' revolt' (Reay 1990), in contrast to 1830, as favoured by the Hammonds. This curious episode, one of the most desperate rebellions since 1745, has attracted two very conflicting interpretations. First, that it was a very localised uprising of simple and incredulous labourers led by the lunatic 'Sir William Courtenay', actually the humble-born John Tom from Cornwall, whose charisma and claims to be Christ attracted a limited following around Hernhill in Kent (P. G. Rogers 1961). Such an interpretation cannot be dismissed lightly and does call into question the political awareness and the broader horizons so emphasised by Wells and Charlesworth. Equally, the fact that thirty or so people were willing to follow a madman speaks volumes as to the depths of despair and anguish that the poor were suffering.

For two days Courtney and his increasingly reluctant followers marched forty-eight miles around an area of Kent which had previously witnessed anti-Poor Law protests in 1835. Although the march was designed to attract further recruits, he in fact lost followers along the way. Just what Courtney was hoping to achieve was never made very clear. Reay's argument that he set out on a messianic quest to bring in a new world order and end the oppression of the poor appears feasible, although his followers probably had the more limited ambition of altering the New Poor Law. After killing a constable, the group was met by a hundred soldiers who opened fire on them before the Riot Act could be read. In all, eight were killed.

For Reay, however, Bosenden Wood was not a unique event in so far as the social and economic contexts which generated this desperate fight could have been replicated across much of Southern England. This resentment was transformed into a vindictive guerrilla-style war that was partially masked by a temporary upturn in agriculture at the end of the 1830s. But this 'background noise' arguably went beyond the endemic arson attacks of the 1840s, described by Jones and Archer, to include all manner of crime as protest. Those of sheep stealing, poaching and petty thieving appear to have been directly linked to the labourers' abortive battle against the Poor Law Amendment Act, although care should be taken in attributing too much social significance to sheep stealing, as some of it could have been the result of organised crime, the activities of greedy farmers and butchers. However, when all is said and done, a protest element remains (Peacock 1974; Rule and Wells 1997: 237–53).

Many of these rural criminals-cum-rebels were young unmarried labourers, different in age composition and status from the convicted rioters of Swing and the New Poor Law disturbances, who were frequently observed to be around thirty years old, industrious, honest and respectable (Hobsbawm and Rudé 1973: 209). The New Poor Law increased rural crime and protest because in practice guardians discriminated against the young casual workers who were offered the workhouse when unemployed. After the first flush of the implementation of the New Poor Law, married men continued to receive outdoor relief for the simple reason that placing them in the workhouse was too expensive. Guardians – rightly as it turned out – assumed that the masculine pride of young labourers prevented them from accepting indoor relief; they preferred instead to poach, steal and work irregularly as best they could. Whilst the young men remained literally the torchbearers in the years after 1840, the remainder of the rural labouring poor remained supportive through their refusal to inform on them whenever trouble flared up in their parish.

3
Food riots

Food riots were the most common and widespread forms of popular collective action during the eighteenth century, accounting for two of every three disturbances. Major outbreaks occurred in 1709–10, 1727–9, 1739–40, 1756–7, 1766–8, 1772–3, 1783–4, 1794–6, 1800–1, 1810–13 and 1816–18, declining rapidly thereafter – the Celtic fringe excepted – to be replaced by other forms of protest. Historians have probably subjected this form of consumer protest to greater and closer analysis than any other form of popular protest and, as a result, the seemingly straightforward food riot has become an event of enormous complexity and variety. The so-called economic reductionist equation of high corn prices equalling a food riot offers only a partial explanation for the timing and occurrence of such events. Furthermore, many food riots were not solely concerned with the price of grain but were frequently related to issues of supply, of grain being exported out of a region during periods of scarcity and of farmers hoarding grain in order to create artificial shortages. The food riot could therefore be directed against a variety of people, from farmers to middlemen and millers, to shopkeepers and grocers, and could take on many forms. The objective was, however, always the same, to ensure a greater supply of food for the community. This was achieved more often than not through threats of violence, rather than actual physical violence to persons, through food seizures, and through appeals to local authorities, who – it must be said – frequently sided with the crowd for a variety of reasons, fear not necessarily being the prevailing motive. The many layers of the food riot have been progressively stripped down and examined. In the process, E. P. Thompson's thesis of the 'moral economy' (1971) has proved enormously influential to our understanding not only of the food riot, but also of other forms of popular action.

Timing and location of food rioting

The years between 1780 and 1820 were generally ones of high wheat prices brought on by poor harvests, inclement weather and most crucially the war with France, which interrupted trade. Britain had by this time become an importer of grain. Whilst the harvest failures of 1795–6 and 1800–1 were undoubtedly serious and devastating to all who experienced them, they were not famines; however, such a conclusion may hinge on the definitions of and distinction between starvation and famine (Wells 1988: 54). The general view among historians, as expressed by Stevenson, was that these 'manifestations of consumer consciousness', which were often grocery riots concerning non-staple foods, did not bring in their train huge jumps in mortality rates (Stevenson 1989: 32) of the magnitude experienced in Ireland in the late 1840s. Wells, however, in agreement with other historians such as Oddy, argues that famine and starvation are 'two quite distinct phenomena', and that many deaths during a famine are not 'directly attributable to starvation' (Wells 1988: 54; Oddy 1983: 68–72).

Table 1 shows the average wheat prices over the war years and it clearly suggests that there was a relationship between prices and riots. But the annual average prices hide enormous monthly and even weekly variations which have led historians to conclude that riots did not coincide with the peaking of prices (Wells 1988: 77; Booth 1977: 88). In the North West, for example, cold and wet weather affected the wheat and potato crops whilst oats actually improved on the previous year. The failure of the former crops raised demand and hence prices for the latter which peaked in March 1796 (Booth 1977: 87–8). Most riots had, however, occurred in July and August 1795 when prices had risen very sharply. A similar pattern can be seen at the end of the century, when a wet summer was followed by a very cold winter and a very hot summer in 1800. Virtually all grain crops and the potato harvest were seriously down in yields, and prices more than doubled between 1798 and October 1800. Wheat prices peaked nationally in March

Table 1. *Average price of wheat in England and Wales 1780–1822 in shillings per imperial quarter*

Major outbreaks of rioting occurred during the years in italic.

	£	s		£	s		£	s
1780	36	9	*1795*	*75*	*2*	*1810*	*106*	*5*
1781	46	0	*1796*	*78*	*7*	*1811*	*95*	*3*
1782	49	3	1797	53	9	*1812*	*126*	*6*
1783	*54*	*3*	1798	51	10	*1813*	*109*	*9*
1784	*50*	*4*	1799	69	0	1814	74	4
1785	*43*	*1*	*1800*	*113*	*10*	1815	65	7
1786	40	0	*1801*	*119*	*6*	*1816*	*78*	*6*
1787	42	5	1802	69	10	*1817*	*96*	*11*
1788	46	4	1803	58	10	*1818*	*86*	*3*
1789	52	9	1804	62	3	1819	74	6
1790	54	9	1805	89	9	1820	67	10
1791	48	7	1806	79	1	1821	56	1
1792	43	0	1807	75	4	1822	44	7
1793	49	3	1808	84	4			
1794	*52*	*3*	1809	97	4			

Source: Adapted from B. Mitchell and P. Deane, 1971, 488–9. I am grateful to Cambridge University Press for permission to reproduce this table.

1801 at 156 shillings a quarter, a figure well in excess of the annual average (Stevenson 1989: 30), but most food disturbances broke out in September 1800, a month which recorded the second lowest average monthly price for that year. The crucial point was that prices were rising very rapidly after the harvest just when the public would have expected them to continue falling. The poor, therefore, suspected underhand dealings by middlemen or hoarding by farmers, creating artificial or manmade scarcities as opposed to natural shortages, which the poor were able to comprehend and accept to some extent (Bohstedt 1983: 17–18). Whilst Stevenson argues that it is the steepness and sharpness of the price rises which set off food riots, this relationship is not replicated in 1804–5 or 1808–9; both periods coincided with general decreases in all forms of riotous behaviour. Bohstedt concedes that riots did coincide with sudden price rises as in September 1795, but such a relationship does not hold good for the spring months of that year, when riots occurred during a period of only gradual price increases. Overall, he has concluded that there 'is no significant relationship between all riots and wheat prices' (ibid.: 18) and that the relationship between food riots and prices was evident but not strong. There was, in other words, no simple cause and effect or what has been called 'rational response' by hungry rioters to dearth. However, it is surely no coincidence that food rioting declined rapidly as a nationwide phenomenon after 1818, when wheat prices fell and agriculture entered a long-term depression until the 1850s. Food prices are an important element, though by no means the only one, in understanding the timing of food riots.

The geography of food riots during this period has similarly proved problematic and open to dispute, although a consensus is emerging on a number of points, not least the relative calm of London and its million inhabitants, whom the authorities ensured were adequately fed even though grain prices fluctuated as much here as elsewhere (Stevenson 1992: 123). It has been estimated that only 4 per cent of all London's riots between 1790 and 1810 were related to food (Bohstedt 1983: 14), one of which included the mobbing of the king in 1795 with cries of 'bread' (Stevenson 1974: 51). This and the 1810 week-long disorder passed off without serious harm to anyone or any property. If London was so well supplied, why then did the price of grain not fall? One unsubstantiated explanation for the relative tranquillity of the capital places the emphasis on timely relief by the authorities and the absence of the 'moral economy' ideology that was so important in the provinces (Bohstedt 1983: 208–9). London aside, our understanding of the geographical concentration of food riots has improved over the years. A table of their distribution between 1795–6 and 1816–18 produced in 1974 needs to be set against the more recent maps, as indeed do the conclusions drawn from them (Stevenson 1974: 36; Charlesworth 1983: 63–71, 94–107).

One pattern identified early on was the apparent migration of riots from Southern and Eastern counties in the earlier decades of the eighteenth century to the Northern and Midland counties in 1800–1. This trend continued during the 1810–12 riots, when industrial and manufacturing towns were the primary troublespots (Stevenson 1974: 45–6). For the climatic year of 1795 Stevenson listed eight disturbances for the whole of the North, rising to ten in 1800–1 (ibid.: 36). Further research showed how wide of the mark these figures were and, by implication, it showed the perils of coming to conclusions about the geographical spread of riots. Twenty-three riots in the North West have been enumerated for 1795–6 and a further seventeen in 1800–1 (Booth 1977: 89). During both episodes industrial and manufacturing towns such as Manchester, Oldham, Bolton, Bury and Blackburn were affected, which suggests that Stevenson's claim that food rioting was still mainly located in the South East and the Midlands in 1795–6 was overstated. No doubt further research into other regions – not least the North East, which is something of 'black hole' when it comes to food disturbances – may bring to light new patterns. A consensus has emerged on a pattern that had long been evident in food disturbances and that continued into the early nineteenth century, namely the importance of communications and supply networks, not least ports, market centres and transshipment points on the canals. Such towns, often small, were the export centres to the burgeoning urban areas. Oxford, for example, a riot-prone town at the best of times, was joined by canal to the Midlands in 1790 and the food riots five years later can be understood in the context of grain being shipped out not just to London as before, but also to the West Midlands (Thwaites 1996: 152). Other grain-exporting centres like East Anglia experienced riots by men and women desperate to keep the grain in their localities.

The West Country, well away from such canal networks, experienced its own peculiar geography of rioting. Devon, it has been claimed, was one of the most riotous counties in eighteenth-century England, experiencing at least forty-three riots in 1795–6 and 1800–1 (Bohstedt 1983: 27). These were concentrated in the more densely populated southern and eastern parishes. Size of community and its propensity to riot were closely correlated since it was found that 90 per cent of the riots occurred in twenty-three communities of more than 1,500 people (Charlesworth 1983: 116–18). Cornwall, which was slightly less productive, likewise experienced riotous behaviour at its small coastal ports and in some of the larger market communities. In years of dearth the county failed to produce enough to feed its own population, let alone export grain to London. In such circumstances the relatively infertile interior of the county, which was home to a mainly non-agricultural population, was in serious trouble; this led to 'invasions' that occurred when tin and copper miners and others moved from the countryside to the ports and markets in search of food (Stevenson 1992: 121–2; Rule 1992: 199; Wells 1988: 100).

The fact that many food riots occurred in largely rural counties and hardly at all in London should not mislead us into believing these were agricultural riots. Food disturbances were urban-based and frequently the work of town artisans and non-agricultural workers, although they could be the result of non-agricultural workers from outlying villages 'invading' market towns. This was particularly true of Cornish miners and rural cloth workers (Charlesworth 1983: 63; Rule 1986: 351). Farmworkers and their families very rarely engaged in such episodes for the simple reason that they had better and more regular access to food, either purchasing it directly from farmers at favourable rates or, if the worst came to the worst, stealing it. Moreover, changes in poor relief systems which tied allowances to the size of labourers' families and the price of bread or wheat provided a basic safety net for many (Stevenson 1989: 34). There was one exception, and that was in East Anglia in 1816, where there was a complex series of riots since labelled the 'Bread or Blood' Riots because of the cry set off by the protesters. However they do display one close similarity with the earlier food riots in the North West in 1812 where such activities were mixed up with Luddism. The Fenland towns of Ely, Littleport and Downham and their hinterlands experienced a combination of machine breaking, food rioting and wage strikes involving farmworkers who had been more completely proletarianised than labourers in other locales (Peacock 1965).

The food rioter

Identifying food rioters can be a difficult undertaking, given the paucity of surviving evidence and the brevity of reports which sometimes refer only to the 'poor'. Such general descriptive terms should not lead one to assume that it was the very poor, those on the absolute margins of society and survival, who played a prominent part in the disturbances, although their presence was occasionally remarked upon (Stevenson 1992: 126). It would appear that the food riot was composed of a representative cross-section of trades that were found in the region in question. For example, copper miners in Cornwall were the main riot force who marched into neighbouring market towns. In like manner colliers in virtually all the affected coalfields except the North East played a leading role, particularly the famously troublesome Kingswood colliers (Malcolmson 1983: 118–22). Local craftsmen, particularly in the textile trades, were perhaps most prominent where their industries were in decline or close to extinction, especially in Essex in the 1790s (Charlesworth 1983: 69) and Devon (Bohstedt 1983: 46). As Booth has shown, though, the burgeoning cotton towns of Lancashire were not immune either. Typically, the protesters were very much part, and often a respectable one at that, of their community. Reports of outsiders causing mayhem and havoc were rare, though canal navigators and navvies did figure occasionally. Perhaps the most surprising participants were the militia and volunteer corps whose role it was to suppress or at least control these very disturbances. In Devon many refused to act against rioters during the 1790s. Some went further when they provided 'a county network for riot' and leadership for the riots of 1800–1 (Bohstedt 1983: 49–50). Their social status and position were identical to those of the rioters and thus they suffered in a similar manner during the shortages. In East Anglia, the 122nd Regiment marched into Wells marketplace with bayonets fixed and ordered food at lower prices (Stevenson 1974: 47). Similar episodes along the South Coast ensured that the government took extra care to provision them at fixed prices so as to ensure their loyalty.

All studies of food riots have observed and commented upon the presence and role of women in these disturbances. 'The wives, widows and daughters of the poor' at Honiton in 1800 demanded food (Stevenson 1974: 49); 'an assemblage of wrong-headed women' and 'a great number of raggetty women' at Lancaster in 1800 are just some of the descriptions (Booth 1977: 98). Were the Hammonds correct in regarding 1795 as the 'year of the revolt of the housewives'; were the women the movers and shakers, the leaders and the predominant participants in such events? No historian has suggested such leading roles for women, although Booth has probably gone further than most by claiming that they were more numerous than men and particularly active. This point has been confirmed by Bohstedt's study of Manchester, where he concluded that the female composition of the crowd explained its disorderly behaviour (Bohstedt 1988: 94). Clearly, male historians have taken to the idea of the angry female food rioter, for the notion of the enraged, impassioned woman heedless of the legal consequences and determined to get a solution to the problem of over-expensive or scarce food has been largely accepted by one of Bohstedt's main critics on this issue (E. P. Thompson 1991: 335–6).

Returning to the main question of women's prominence in food riots, Bohstedt felt the necessity to raise the 'Aunt Sally' of women's domination in food riots – what he terms 'the myth of feminine food riot' – in order to destroy it with some questionable statistical analysis and arguments about women's role in the market place. From his sample of 617 riots between 1790 and 1810, he found that 240 were related to food. Breaking this figure down, he has attempted to categorise food riots by gender with the following figures: riots in which women were dominant – thirty-five, women and men – forty-two, men only – eighty-one, and gender unknown – eighty-two (Bohstedt 1988: 91). These figures are to a large extent meaningless: in 34 per cent of riots he has no idea of the gender composition of the crowd, and in the remaining 66 per cent there is no way of determining whether men or women predominated because the reports are too short. Riots, furthermore, evolve. People are drawn into them or they may even be sent away when the military arrive. His methodology is in this particular instance suspect (E. P. Thompson 1991: 307–14) and, as Thompson observed, a twenty-year sample of food riot incidents taken in the final years of a 200-year-long tradition may not be representative. Food riots evolved over the years and their form altered from place to place as Bohstedt has so persuasively shown; and in the case of women's involvement it is feasible to accept that Lancastrian women and others from 'boom' industrialising areas were significantly more violent than those from the smaller market towns of the West Country (Bohstedt 1988: 106–11).

The other line of attack in demolishing the myth of the female food rioter concerns her roles as housewife, homemaker, shopper or 'partner in the household economy'. Apart from the problem of anachronistic language, historians should take care not to allow political correctness to cloud their historical faculties and academic judgements. Whilst more work may well be needed, enough

archival material survives which suggests that women were prominent in the marketplace as sellers and stallholders, and most importantly as purchasers, which meant they would have been especially
sensitive to price increases and deterioration in quality.

The form of the food riot

The term 'food riot' hides a multiplicity of different forms of popular crowd actions, which ranged from the entirely peaceful parading
through the town to arson attacks on mills. By far the most common
form of protest was concerned with the regulation of prices, *taxation
populaire* or price fixing, which was imposed on bakers, middlemen
and millers depending on whether bread or flour was the object of
the crowd's interest. Even grocery items such as meat, cheese and
butter could suffer the same fate as the staples of wheat and po-
tatoes. There were considerable variations on this theme of price
regulation, ranging from the crowd's seizure of goods which were
then publicly auctioned, to seizure by the crowd who then sold it
among themselves. In most instances they set what they felt was a
'just' or 'fair' price and handed their money over to the dealer at the
price which they had set. Only rarely do we find the crowd pilfering
and looting goods and only occasionally did they scatter and damage the food. The latter was done by way of punishment, which
suggests that some disturbances had evolved beyond simple protests about food prices or availability. Some regions experienced
disturbances that attempted to prevent the movement of grain.
These included grain-growing areas that themselves suffered shortages in 1795 and 1800–1, such as East Anglia and North Wales, and
the Midland granary region close to the canals and navigable water-
ways. All these have been clearly mapped by Charlesworth (1983:
98–103). Quite the opposite trend could also spark riots, not least
the suspected hoarding of grain by farmers in the rural areas. Along
the South Coast, crowds with ropes and halters moved from farm to
farm forcing farmers to bring their grain to market, where the
populace was given preferential treatment over cornfactors both in
terms of price and provision. Both this feeling of movement, of
miners moving to towns in search of grain and townsfolk scouring
the countryside for hidden granaries, and the role of ritual in the

crowd's behaviour have been examined. Bread placed on poles and bedecked in black crepe, musical bands and, on occasion, effigy burnings give the impression that the crowd tended to act with considerable discipline, although a new and deeper anger has been discerned by the end of the century (E. P. Thompson 1971: 135). Food rioters did not knowingly kill anyone even though, at the last estimate, thirty or so of their number were shot or executed. During the eighteenth century, crowds, it would seem, were more threatening and less disciplined in London and the larger conurbations (Stevenson 1992: 130). In the former, a mill was attacked and fired and in the North West it would appear that food riots blended comfortably into Luddism after 1810 (ibid.: 128; Charlesworth 1983: 104–6). By the early decades of the nineteenth century it is, at times, difficult to separate food rioting from other popular actions and disturbances related to political radicalism and trade unionism (Booth 1977: 100–4). Historians should therefore resist the temptation to pigeon-hole each type of popular protest activity as being independent and separate from other forms and disputes. One form does not necessarily evolve into another form of protest: they can run concurrently, consecutively or both.

The 'moral economy'

No study of the eighteenth century has been so influential as E. P. Thompson's 'The Moral Economy of the English Crowd' (1971). This essay has probably attracted an appreciative group of historians far in excess of its detractors, some of whom Thompson felt had misunderstood the core idea of the moral economy. He therefore re-explored the concept in *Customs in Common* (1991). He was concerned with what he called the *mentalité* of the crowd, its set of ideas and beliefs, values and expectations of what constituted proper and traditional behaviour with regard to marketing, milling and baking (ibid.: 260).

The moral economy has also been examined by Outhwaite (1990: 54–6) to some extent, as it was operating well before 1780, but later work has been heavily critical of the concept (Bohstedt 1992). One of its key characteristics was the discipline of the crowd, but just what is meant by discipline? Numerous examples abound from the dearth years of the 1790s and 1800–1 of violent crowd action against property, and the issuing of dire threats to individual bakers and farmers. These were not, however, examples of mindless mobs running out of control. They were examples of crowds selecting targets or individuals who were, in their opinion, cheating the moral economy. Violence could be permissible in such circumstances, and it has been argued that there was a pattern and a shape within the popular action that was understandable to both the authorities and the participants. Bohstedt's phrase 'orderly disorder' is appropriate in such circumstances, as indeed is his notion of the 'protocols of riot'. There were rules to the game which could occasionally break down or evolve and change over time. It would be overstating the case to say that in Devon these were well understood, yet all but jettisoned in Manchester, as Bohstedt has argued. If we were to accept Bohstedt's model, the riot was learned behaviour in which the crowd had only to gather and the local authorities would grant some kind of concession which would uphold the public peace and preserve social order. All this appears rather tame and too orderly for the descriptive word 'riot' to be appropriate. And what are historians to make of the crowds which scattered the grain or flour rather than distributing it at a 'fair' price? Has the moral economy broken down or is this action a punishment directed by the crowd at a particular person who was not playing the game? In these cases the punishment can be viewed as part of the moral economy according to Charlesworth (1993: 208).

The moral economy does not set out to explain why food riots occurred in certain districts. Rather, it aims to explain the behaviour of the crowd and its attitude to forestallers, engrossers, dealers and anyone else suspected of cheating and imposing free market economic values – illegitimate practices in other words – on the basics of life. But this does not mean that the crowd was totally opposed to the laws of supply and demand, which they understood well enough to fix high prices in times of scarcity on food which they had liberated (Wells 1983: 84). What the crowd found unacceptable and immoral were the artificial scarcities created by hoarders and wholesalers who withheld grain from the market. But it has been noted that industrial workers, in some cases, believed that food riots were harmful to the people in the medium to long term in so far as the suppliers would be frightened off and send their grain to quieter

markets (Bohstedt 1983: 55). In that sense the crowd's enforcement of the moral economy could lead to disaster (Wells 1988:
230). Whilst E. P. Thompson chastised Wells for alarmism and
exaggeration, he did allow the point that one region's moral economy could lead to another region's scarcity (1991: 289–90).

The other side of the moral economy coin was crucially the
reaction of the authorities to the crowd's demands and actions.
Evidence abounds on the fact that local authorities subscribed to
the plebeian values and were willing to prosecute sellers who used
faulty weights or adulterated food, and they frequently set a 'fair
price' and forced producers to market in the 1790s, often against
the wishes of the central government (E. P. Thompson 1991: 279).
They did so partly out of ideological belief, but also because they
were 'prisoners of the people' (ibid.: 199) and were desperately
trying to keep paternalism alive in order to preserve their superior
status (ibid.: 301). A riot, in other words, concentrated the local
authorities' minds wonderfully. The overall situation was becoming
more complex by the 1790s, but many authorities continued to
react in the manner expected of them and thus food rioting remained a popular and successful mode of behaviour into the nineteenth century (ibid.: 293–4). Their high success rate, it has been
suggested, owed less to the general legitimacy imbued in the
crowd's actions and more to the successful time-tested tactics of
food rioting.

Thompson's model does not explain why food riots broke out
where they did. This has proved to be the most difficult of questions
to answer. Perhaps the most interesting and fullest attempt has been
provided by Bohstedt in *Riots and Community Politics* (1983) in
which he argued that the historian had to understand the local social
framework and relationships between social groups within the community, since this could be suggestive of the type of direct popular
action carried out in that community. For Bohstedt there were
basically three types of community (if London is set aside): namely
boom industrial towns such as Manchester, small market towns
found in counties such as Devon, and rural villages. The classic
food riot tended to be located in small market towns, whereas in
industrial towns with a high influx of migrants and a greater social
distance between the people and the patricians, no consensus existed. Here, riots tended to be disorderly and more threatening,

which suggested that the moral economy had broken down. Consequently, they were repressed with greater energy. Under this model those living in the countryside were so totally overwhelmed by the power and control exercised by the landed gentry as to make collective protest a reckless tactic. This may well oversimplify regional variations, though; Cornish miners, for example, did not appear to have been easily overawed or browbeaten by the authorities. As has been suggested earlier, the distinctions drawn by Bohstedt between Manchester – 'the city of strangers' – and Devon are probably overdrawn, since Mancunian justices of the peace frequently intervened in the economy to enforce paternalist regulations. Even the local press in the supposed home of laissez faire were highly critical of marketing practices such as forestalling and engrossing (Charlesworth 1993: 208–9). As with all historical explanations, the moral economy cannot provide answers to all the questions relating to food rioting. But when it is taken in conjunction with the analyses of high prices, geography, social composition, size of the community, distance from food-producing areas, access to communications and tradition, such a combination provides some kind of explanation of food rioting as a phenomenon.

Slightly less mysterious is the decline of food rioting in the nineteenth century. It would appear that the food riot tradition and culture, which had taken centuries to evolve, peaked in the period between 1795 and 1801 and then rapidly died away to the fringes of the British Isles. However, it is important to note that food disturbances were not simply replaced by other forms of collective action such as machine breaking or early trade unionism, since these latter forms could coincide with food and price riots (Booth 1977: 104; Stevenson 1992: 137–8). Protest that had been effective in small communities increasingly became less so in the larger towns and urbanising regions where the authorities became less and less sympathetic to crowd actions and the moral economy. Consequently, they tended to meet direct action with repression (Charlesworth 1993: 211). By this time the fear of the masses, of political radicalism and the growing success of Smithian economics meant that the poor were not to be negotiated with. As important an explanation for the decline (though a much more prosaic one) was the absence of food crises in England after the Napoleonic wars when prices slumped. The most immediate concerns for the working classes became the figurative, rather than literal, bread-and-butter issues of employment and wages. There were, of course, exceptions as food riots were still being experienced in 1847 and as late as 1867 in the South West (Charlesworth 1983: 108–11; Storch 1982).

4
Industrial protest

Industrial protest was probably second only to consumer protest in the eighteenth century but soon surpassed the latter by the second decade of the nineteenth century, when the most famous episodes and examples of direct action and industrial sabotage bequeathed a new word to the English language – Luddism. The word, now commonly associated with opposition to new technology, certainly possessed, in part, that meaning in 1811 when the Luddite disturbances first broke out in Nottingham. As a movement, however, Luddism appears to have been much more complex in character and, as a consequence, has been a subject of considerable debate. Moreover, although Luddism is undoubtedly the most widely researched phenomenon of industrial protest, it represents just one facet of a continuum of labour struggles and tactics. Early works by the Webbs and the Hammonds, though useful in providing detail and powerful description, have largely been superseded by the works of Rule, Randall, Thompson and Thomis, to name but a few. Their research has located industrial protest more precisely in its community contexts rather than simply placing it in the socio-economic context of industrialisation or modernisation. Modern scholars, by placing these struggles within their communities, have been able to show how the wealth of communal resources, craft traditions and solidarities enabled workforces to prolong disputes. In addition, the reaction of local authorities was as important in prolonging or ending these disputes. The fact that industries were regional and dominated by one or two occupations was both a strength and a weakness for protesters. Moreover, by viewing protest in the context of location, the importance of chronology and tradition have become increasingly evident. In times of extreme tension and distress, such as towards the end of the Napoleonic wars, industrial protest could, it has been argued by some historians, easily become politicised (Charlesworth *et al.* 1996: 32; Dinwiddy 1979). This too has been disputed, but such disagreements should at least alert the student to the dangers of compartmentalising too securely the various forms of protest. Food rioting, machine breaking and political radicalism might well have been present in the same dispute.

Pre-Luddite protest

Industrial protest encompassed many different kinds of activities. Popular actions ranged from the legal petitioning of local authorities, justices of the peace, mayors and Parliament, to strikes and the more obvious forms of rowdy behaviour of mass meetings such as rioting, effigy burnings and rough music, to outright terrorism in the form of assassination, the sending of threatening letters, arson, machine breaking and other forms of sabotage and property damage. It should be emphasised that, as in food rioting, few people were killed by the protesters, although more of them were shot or executed by the authorities than in consumer protests.

Traditional studies have tended to search out the origins of trade unions since history has shown that this was the way forward for effective working-class action and organisation. Thus, the early studies not only placed an emphasis on the existence of early combinations which were common among the craft industries in London, they also underplayed the role of industrial violence and direct action. These latter activities have been branded as the 'crude barbarism' (Musson 1972: 15) of disorganised and blinkered reactionaries who were vainly attempting to halt progress and modernisation. Even Hobsbawm in his pioneering essay 'Machine Breakers' (1968: 5–22) argued that this form of 'collective bargaining by riot' indicated that trade unionism was either weak or absent. Thus, for labour historians, the notion of an evolutionary development from violence to permanent continuous worker associations was axiomatic, and this evolutionary scale provided important benchmarks by which worker consciousness, solidarity and strength could be measured.

A number of issues and problems arise from this interpretative approach. One concerns the evidence consulted by Dobson, for example, who set out to show that peaceful conflict and worker organisation were extensive in the eighteenth century. He found 400 labour disputes in the British Isles between 1717 and 1800, of which 138 occurred between 1781 and 1800 (Dobson 1980: 18–22). Many were London-based, occurring among some of the well-established craft organisations which were not necessarily typical of the provinces where, in the Webbs' view, workers' combinations could be more short-lived and 'ephemeral' (Charlesworth *et al.* 1996: 1–2). Rule has modified this interpretation with his observation that these early trade unions were often more geographically widespread and 'effective' than previous labour historians have allowed, but that they were not 'consistently effective' (Rule and Malcolmson 1993: 117). In addition, Charlesworth has made the powerful and valid point that historians should resist imposing the model of Victorian trade unions on the eighteenth century, since protest often arose in a community context where divisions between 'work' and 'life' were limited in the era before factory organisation (Charlesworth *et al.* 1996: 2–3). Moreover, many regions had traditions of a successful rebellious culture which could range from the ubiquitous food riot and the turnpike riot to the mobbing of individuals – riding the stang for example – directed at those people who had broken community norms (see above, 14).

Recent research has uncovered a rich culture and tradition of industrial protest in provincial England, which suggests that industrial violence and direct action were tactics indicative of community strength and not weakness (Randall 1982). The early success of eighteenth-century labour movements lay, according to Hobsbawm, in machine breaking (1968: 6), destruction of property and rioting. This kind of sabotage he famously termed 'collective bargaining by riot'. It was a traditional element of industrial conflict and labour negotiation and did not imply any particular antipathy to mechanisation as such. It was, however, a highly selective method of bringing industry to a halt and imposing solidarity on the workforce. This can be seen in the ways miners wrecked the winding gear at pit heads, thus preventing either anyone from working or employers from bringing in blackleg labour. It was an effective bargaining technique which brought employers to the metaphorical negotiating table very rapidly indeed. The second type of machine breaking identified by Hobsbawm was concerned with hostility to new labour-saving machinery and this was, in his opinion, a far less successful tactic since the former could not hope to halt the advance of technical progress (ibid.: 17).

One industry and region which experienced persistent popular industrial sabotage in the era before the Luddites was the woollen industry of the West Country. Almost every new form of machinery connected with this industry, from spinning in 1776 through to looms and shearing frames, was met with anger in the form of riots and attacks on property. Even the flying shuttle, which had been in use in Lancashire and Yorkshire from the 1760s, met with riots at Trowbridge in 1792 and these successfully slowed down the introduction of these machines (Charlesworth *et al.* 1996: 24–6). Although it was their labour-saving qualities which angered the Wiltshire and Somerset communities, Randall and Charlesworth have noted that they were much disliked where wives of textile workers were threatened with redundancy, whereas wives of agricultural labourers failed to offer the same level of resistance. Why this should be the case appears to lie in the fact that textile communities were more cohesive and possessed a strong sense of solidarity (Randall and Charlesworth 1996: 28).

The most famous episode in this region was the Wiltshire Outrages of 1802, in which the highly skilled and status-conscious shearmen were threatened with redundancy from gig mills and shearing frames (Randall 1982, 1991). The events of the West Country were, as it turned out, to act as a bridgehead between eighteenth-century machine breaking and the Luddite disturbances of 1812. Randall's studies detail how erroneous it is to treat machine wrecking and trade unionism as separate and, by implication, opposite tactical entities (1982: 284). The shearmen attempted to halt the spread of gig mills and shearing frames in three ways: by the trade union technique of strikes, by direct action and violence or the threat of violence, and by going to court and to Parliament to argue the illegality of such machinery. What Randall found – and this contradicts the works of Thomis – was that the Wiltshire shearmen were not only unionised but that they were in a federal-style union with their Yorkshire colleagues. They had, in other words, a strong union structure with which to back industrial action, as indeed they had in 1802 when there were three strikes in Wiltshire. Even though they had considerable public support and sympathy and even benign magisterial interference, the strike weapon was ineffective in getting rid of machinery, despite the fact that the Combination Acts were in force. There occurred discriminatory industrial violence which followed a pattern of increasing pressure on clothiers. This began with the sending of threatening letters and arson attacks and, if these warnings were not heeded, ended with attacks on carefully selected machinery. Although these attacks were limited in number, suggesting that there were not that many gig mills to destroy, the shearmen still had the law courts and parliamentary petitions as further tactics. Thompson's 'moral economy' model has been successfully adapted by Randall in this context of industrial conflict (Randall 1988). In this case the ideological struggle was between an economy based on regulatory legislation concerning apprenticeships and the use of machinery, for example, and one based on free trade and non-interference from Parliament. The latter viewpoint, upheld by large clothiers, prevailed when regulatory legislation was suspended in 1803 and then repealed in 1809, a decision which was to have enormous implications for the Yorkshire woollen industry and Luddism (E. P. Thompson 1968: 578). In the West Country the violence of the early nineteenth century slowed down the introduction of machinery until 1816, when the final acts of resistance occurred; by this time the woollen industry in this region was close to extinction. What the Wiltshire outrages show above all else are the dangers of separating trade union organisation and direct action and treating them as distinct activities in which the latter occurred where the former was weak or absent. It is possible to argue, as Randall has done, that the Wiltshire outrages were successful in a limited way. These protests did, after all, slow down the introduction of machinery, unlike in neighbouring Gloucestershire, where shearmen unsuccessfully opted for peaceful and legal resistance. However, one cannot get away from the fact that the Wiltshire industry died because it was uncompetitive with Yorkshire.

The outrages occurred shortly after the passing of the Combination Acts of 1799 and 1800 which have been described as a 'much misunderstood' landmark in trade union history (Rule 1992: 209). Originally, commentators argued that through this legislation the state had totally surrendered to employers, who could now repress trade unions unhindered. Whilst this extremely bleak interpretation was rejected by George (1927), who regarded the Combination Acts as a 'negligible instrument of repression', her views have come under close scrutiny (Orth 1991: 43–67). More recent interpretations have argued that the legislation was directed at 'workmen as a class' rather than at individual crafts and unions. The legislation also suggests that government had undergone a significant change of attitude in so far as all trade unions were now seen as potentially dangerous forces which could undermine the political system. The 1790s had, after all, been a crisis-strewn decade of war with revolutionary France, high prices and food shortages, and of most relevance in this context, a large number of successful strikes and combinations (Stevenson 1992: 160).

Although prior to 1799 much legislation existed that made trade unions and their activities illegal through laws on conspiracy, breach of contract and individual statutes relating to particular industries, the Combination Acts made prosecution quicker and simpler, and were all encompassing. They made an important contribution to the repressive power of the authorities as well as adding to the intimidatory atmosphere experienced at this time. But their main purpose, according to the Webbs (1911) and Rule (Rule and Malcolmson 1993: 118 20), was to make workers accept the rule of their employers. Disorder and indiscipline in the form of strikes were no longer to be tolerated and even though there was, as yet, no link between trade unionism and political radical subversion, the government regarded the unions as subversive in their own right (ibid.: 122). It would, however, appear that the laws were used selectively: the highly organised craft societies of London's skilled labour force were largely unmolested, whereas the more northerly and expanding trades concerned with textiles and mining which possessed massed groups of manufacturing workers were probably the primary focus of the new legislation (Laybourn 1992: 16–20). The events of the first decade of the nineteenth century suggest that the Combination Acts failed to prevent Lancashire weavers from rioting and striking in 1808 or the spinners in 1802, 1803 and 1810 (Stevenson 1992: 192–3). Whilst historians are unsure about how often and exactly where the acts were resorted to, it could be argued that their most important and unintended effect was to politicise unions such as the Lancashire spinners who, because of the laws, now had to go underground and operate in a twilight world of subversion already inhabited by political radicals (E. P. Thompson 1968: 546–7). Although it is debatable whether radicals took over the leadership of working-class trade unions, it is indisputable that workers continued to combine, to strike, to attack property and to break machinery in the face of enormous legal obstacles, the most famous episode being Luddism.

Luddism

Although the term 'Luddism' is often employed to describe machine breaking in general, most historians apply it to the very limited period 1811–16 and to the specific geographical areas of Nottingham, Leicestershire and South Derbyshire, the West Riding of Yorkshire and parts of Lancashire and Cheshire in the North West. And whilst it belongs to the well-established tradition of machine wrecking, Thomis has argued that the uniqueness of the second decade of the nineteenth century lies in the widespread geographical distribution and the intensity of the disturbances which were, for him and earlier historians such as Darvall (1969), essentially industrial in character (Thomis 1970: 17). This narrow interpretation had already been rejected by E. P. Thompson (1968: 579–659) who argued that Luddism developed a political dimension that was radical and even revolutionary in tone and content and that, as a consequence, it represented an important step forward in the making of the English working class. Such an interpretation has been accepted and enhanced further by Rule, whose claim that Luddism was 'a guerrilla campaign' (1992: 219) has taken the movement far beyond the narrow industrial-conflict school. The true significance and character of Luddism are therefore disputed, and thus what initially appeared as examples, albeit spectacular ones, of industrial sabotage and direct action may have possessed a darker and more sinister meaning for the state and society in Regency England. In order to examine and clarify the parameters of this debate, it is helpful to place the various episodes in their complex and specific geographic and industrial contexts, whilst at the same time recognising that all three regions were experiencing common economic problems. These general problems included poor harvests and spiralling food prices, unemployment and short-time working leading to wage cuts, and the deregulation of industries through the repeal of old paternalist and restrictive statutes covering such matters as apprenticeships and the use of machinery. It has been argued that Luddism was 'a crisis point in the abrogation of paternalist legislation, and in the imposition of the political economy of laissez faire upon, and against the will and conscience of, the working people' (E. P. Thompson 1968: 594). Investigation of the regions emphasises the fact that Luddism possessed as many differences as it had similarities.

In Nottinghamshire, where both the legendary Ned Ludd and the movement arose, Luddism appears to have conformed most closely to Hobsbawm's model of 'collective bargaining by riot'. In the spring of 1811, framework knitters were already in dispute with their employers over wage cuts and, more crucially, the employment of unskilled apprentices who produced inferior stockings or 'cut ups' on wide frames. Their leader, Gravener Henson, attempted to start legal proceedings against the low-paying employers but met with no success. Consequently, very selective frame breaking in Arnold occurred in March 1811 (Rule 1986: 367; Charlesworth *et al.* 1996: 34). Machine breaking appears to have made a phased return in November and over a much wider area including parts of Derbyshire and Leicestershire. In this phase, lasting into January 1812, a pattern of frame breaking and interludes in which to allow employers to make concessions has been identified (Charlesworth *et al.* 1996: 35). Although the wider 'cut up' frames were initially singled out for destruction, by the peak of January 1812 machine wrecking had become less selective. In all, over 1,000 frames were broken in 100 separate incidents over the eleven-month period. A switch of tactics, brought about by the heavy military presence in Nottingham and Parliament's decision to make machine breaking a capital offence, occurred when the United Committee of Framework Knitters attempted to petition Parliament for legislation to regulate their industry. This proved equally unsuccessful, as the Combination Acts were brought in as a prosecution weapon. Peaceful methods were replaced by a resumption of sporadic frame breaking until 1816.

The Midland disturbances spread north to the West Riding of Yorkshire in January 1812, where Luddism proved to be more complex in character. Here the disturbances were reminiscent of the earlier Wiltshire outrages in so far as the woollen cloth finishers, known as croppers, found their livelihoods threatened by the introduction of gig mills and shearing frames. As an elite, well-organised group, the croppers had successfully resisted mechanisation until 1811, when the large employers began to install machines. Beginning with an arson attack in Leeds, the nocturnal raids on the dressing shops intensified and spread to the Halifax area. The attitudes of both the employers and croppers appear to have been far more extreme and bitter than elsewhere, and this is typified by the deaths of two Luddites attacking Cartwright's mill in April 1812, followed by the attempted assassination of Cartwright himself and the murder of another millowner, William Horsfall. This Luddite violence was sufficient to persuade smaller owners to dismantle their own machines but larger millowners continued with machinery because their mills were well defended. For E. P. Thompson (1968: 616–17), April was the crisis month for Yorkshire Luddism, as violence spread into other parts of the county, took on revolutionary undertones and evolved far beyond machine breaking to include criminal activities such as theft of money and arms. This association between mainstream crime and Luddism is, as will be seen, disputed by Thomis (1970: 17–19) but at the time the authorities were sufficiently persuaded of the link and exacted terrible vengeance at the Yorkshire assizes, where seventeen were executed.

Luddism in Lancashire and Cheshire poses equally challenging problems since its character was not narrowly defined by machine wrecking which was almost incidental to the other activities. In addition to the handloom weavers' attacks on the new powerlooms, warehouses and owners' homes were attacked and in some cases, as at Stockport, by 'General Ludd's wives' who were in fact men dressed as women. Food riots blended into machine-breaking attacks in some instances, but the most distinctive element of the North West Luddite disturbances concerns the political agitation that accompanied other forms of protest. This region was, after all, home to well-established but illegal trade unions and secret weavers' committees which formed a powerful network around Manchester and which co-ordinated the attack in April 1812 on the Manchester Exchange, the venue for a Tory meeting. This proved to be the lighting of the touchpaper in the region. By the end of April it was evident that direct action had failed and those involved in the disturbances appear to have diverged and gone down two separate avenues. The more moderate realised parliamentary reform might be more successful in bringing about change favourable to the working classes, whereas a more revolutionary and extreme strand, it has been claimed, went for arms raids, and drilling and marching on the moors in preparation for the day of reckoning (E. P. Thompson 1968: 622; Charlesworth *et al.* 1996: 42–6).

There were three Luddite regions, as we have seen, with three very different experiences. Is it possible to achieve a consensus on their interpretation? The answer is definitely in the negative for, as Thomis has so correctly written, 'when historians are in agreement about the Luddites, historical controversy will be at an end' (Thomis 1970: 28). E. P. Thompson and Thomis represent the extremes of the interpretative spectrum which contains intervening and more moderate positions held by, for example, Dinwiddy (see below, 53–4). Most but not all early accounts of Luddism agree that it was a manifestation of industrial protest. The most notable exception to this stance came from the work of Frank Peel (1969 edn, originally published 1880), who recalled the Yorkshire Luddites and their oath taking and revolutionary rhetoric through the oral tradition of the region. Later research has in the main supported Peel's work, although errors of detail have been identified. This revolutionary strand to Luddism was largely discounted by Darvall (1969: 317), who rejected the idea of political motivation in favour of local and limited objectives belonging to the respective trades. The Hammonds too placed the phenomenon in an industrial but wider time perspective in which traditional workers, having failed to keep protective and paternalist legislation on the statute books, resorted to machine breaking in a final attempt to maintain or reinstate old customs and laws. Luddism was to them reactionary but neither mindless nor the work of inevitable losers (as the Webbs thought of them). Such a view is not dissimilar from the one expressed by Bythell, who branded smashing powerlooms as not only 'old fashioned' and 'pointless physical violence' (1969: 180) but also as indicative of weak worker organisation. Only when the workers shake off these 'barbaric' methods, it has been argued, and move towards peaceful collective bargaining do they stand any chance of success and, by implication, earn the historians' respect. Even later marxist historians have perceived Luddism in similarly narrow industrial terms in which the Luddites were basically anti-mechanisation in principle.

This limited industrial interpretation was fundamentally and for many irreversibly challenged in 1963 with the publication of *The Making of the English Working Class* in which E. P. Thompson argued that Luddism was a 'quasi-insurrectionary movement' which belonged to the English revolutionary tradition. This was especially pronounced in Yorkshire and Lancashire, less so in the Midlands; yet even here Thompson became embroiled in a debate about the relationship between machine breaking and the more peaceful parliamentary campaign led by Gravener Henson (1968: 924–34). Were they, as Henson and later the Hammonds maintained, entirely separate or were there different tactical approaches operating under the same leadership? For critics of Thompson such as Church and Chapman (1967), there were two groups of protesters present in the Midlands, the more law-abiding and skilled town knitters and the less skilled lower-paid country knitters who resorted to violence whenever the peaceful methods failed. By mapping out the Midland outbreaks, Charlesworth shows that there were distinct phases, fluctuating between negotiating and frame breaking – for example in the third phase in December 1811, when hosiers had been forced to negotiate a settlement over wages. The fourth phase – a machine-breaking one – began at the end of the month to see if further concessions could be wrung from the employers. This phase ended in February 1812 when Parliament made frame breaking a capital offence (Charlesworth *et al.* 1996: 34–7). The presence of thousands of troops no doubt influenced the Nottingham Luddites to return to peaceful constitutional methods and reject the frame-breaking tactic, the latter being resorted to only sporadically over the next five years.

Whilst all protagonists in the debate would agree that Nottinghamshire Luddism contained little political content or activity, there has been serious disagreement about the Northern counties. In Yorkshire – and Lancashire as well – Thompson has emphasised that these regions already possessed a political underground which gave the movement its political character. The actual machine-breaking phase was brief, lasting between January and April 1812 when, according to Thompson, Yorkshire Luddism reached its crisis point with the failure of their attacks on the heavily fortified mills (1968: 646). At this point the political dimension of Luddism increased as the men were becoming more desperate. This politicisation process of industrial grievances can also be seen in the Lancashire disturbances. However, these events were complicated by the presence of food rioting, crime waves, trade union activities and parliamentary reform agitation to such an extent that Thomis believes 'authentic Luddism' may not have been present; rather he sees it representing a 'shapeless protest movement' (1970: 27, 163).

Thomis's criticism of Thompson rests on a number of crucial methodological issues, not least the reading and interpretation of archival sources and the former's very narrow approach of compartmentalising and separating each form of popular protest rather than allowing for the fact that events and tactics could have evolved and developed. But, as Dinwiddy has very reasonably argued, it is difficult to draw a distinction between industrial and political action since they could be and often were the same (1992: 373). Thomis would maintain, however, that Luddism was narrowly defined as machine breaking and that some contemporaries tended to define any protest or wrongdoing as Luddite. Thus, the arms raids and robberies in Yorkshire were, according to him, nothing more or less than criminal acts committed by criminals even though the convicted termed themselves Luddites (Thomis 1970: 18–19).

A more serious and irresolvable argument against Thompson has been concerned with the evidence contained in the reports to the Home Office. Earlier interpretations by the Hammonds and Darvall had totally ignored evidence which suggested ulterior political or revolutionary aims. 'There is no evidence whatsoever,' Darvall wrote, 'of any political motives on the part of the Luddites', 'there was no army, no national organization of the Luddites, no extensive secret conspiracy' (1969: 176–97), thus supporting the Hammonds' view that spies and *agents provocateurs* invented or exaggerated the insurrectionary plans and designs. Thompson's willingness to reread the evidence and, in part, believe it without accepting wilder conspiracy theories put a very different gloss on Luddism. By far the most reasoned and balanced conclusion to this debate has come from Dinwiddy (1979) who re-examined the relationship between Luddism and political agitation, both revolutionary and reformist, in the Northern counties. There was, he argued, considerable working-class activity prior to the 1812 machine breaking and in this respect the reports of the government spy, Bent, can be considered reliable. Unlike Thomis, who felt the Luddites lacked the sophistication to be political, Dinwiddy has argued that the weavers' committees prior to 1812 had already made the connection between the need for parliamentary reform and the redressing of their economic grievances, but he suggests the secret oath taking and the arms thefts may have had limited objectives connected not to insurrection but to machine breaking. In Yorkshire, too, Dinwiddy emphasised the industrial content of the machine-breaking period between January and April 1812 and is willing to concede that ordinary criminals used the cloak of Luddism to pursue their thieving, but he does allow for the existence of evidence which hints at the presence of underground revolutionary groups in the two counties. He therefore rejects Thomis's narrow interpretation but only tentatively supports Thompson in so far as there were revolutionaries present. It is impossible to discern what the relationship, if any, these revolutionaries had with the machine breakers. Of far more importance was the re-emergence of political radicalism in the late summer of 1812 when Major Cartwright visited the North. By early 1813 over 30,000 people in the two counties had signed petitions calling for parliamentary reform (Dinwiddy 1992: 398).Thus, machine breaking was politicised, but was not necessarily replaced by other forms of action such as political reform campaigning and trade unionism. All three could and did exist simultaneously in Lancashire and Yorkshire between 1812 and 1830.

Lest we forget, Luddism by no means disappeared in the North after 1812, since during the depression of 1826 Lancashire probably experienced a more extensive outbreak of machine breaking than in the earlier attacks fifteen years previously. It has been estimated that 1,000 looms were smashed and 21 factories attacked in East Lancashire (Hammond and Hammond 1979; Stevenson 1992: 258). These disturbances, which spread to Manchester by the end of April, have not as yet brought to light any radical political input; rather Stevenson has called them 'a last ditch attempt', 'a gesture of despair' to destroy machinery which the weavers believed was the cause of their misery. As in earlier episodes the weavers won over widespread community support to the extent that a significant minority of those arrested in the Blackburn area belonged to other trades and occupations (Charlesworth *et al.* 1996: 50). Nor did this form of direct action and sabotage die away immediately, for 1829 witnessed yet more attacks on powerlooms in Manchester in what was a kaleidoscope of protest activities that included a highly disciplined variant of the food riot during which there were strikes against butter and milk dealers (Bythell 1969: 180–1), ceremonial parades, arson attacks and strikes. All this indicates the weakness of union organisation among handloom weavers and suggests that industrial violence was by this time a tactic of the doomed or, as Thompson termed them, 'casualties' and 'losers' (ibid.: 190; E. P. Thompson 1968: 13).

By this time less physical methods were being adopted among some of the major trades, not least the cotton spinners led by John Doherty in 1829–30. Historical emphasis has been placed on trade union activity and the attempts to form national organisations like the famous Grand National Consolidated Trade Union of 1833–4 with its Owenite tendencies (Kirby and Musson 1975). Direct action and violence, however, were never completely eradicated nor were such methods always indicative of organisational weakness. In these small-scale actions of intimidation, extra-legal union activity could be unusually effective and hard to eradicate. In his study of militant Oldham, Foster lists many instances of such direct actions between 1831 and 1834: colliers stoning blacklegs, violent picketing, arson attacks during pay disputes and acid attacks on an employer and a manager (Foster 1974: 51). This latter form of personal attack was also utilised during the weavers' disputes in Norwich in the late 1820s and personal violence was much in evidence during the North East miners' dispute in which a magistrate was murdered (Rule 1986: 315; Hammond and Hammond 1979: 33–4). Such violence was, admittedly, becoming increasingly rare, and neither the failures of national and general unionism nor the state repression, as exemplified by the Tolpuddle Martyrs, prevented the quiet and continued growth of trade unionism among skilled and semi-skilled workers, who generally rejected militant direct action in favour, in some cases, of the political organisation and objectives of Chartism. Protest related to industrial issues had generally altered over the years under review, but the changes were neither as dramatic nor as clear-cut as was once thought. However, there can be no denying the fact that by the 1830s the working-class movement was seeking ways of forming permanent and organised associations and unions. In recognising this, industrial sabotage in the form of machine breaking should not be written off as primitive or vandalistic. The research of Randall and Rule has shown that it was controlled and selective, and possessed a history of its own which located it in the relevant communities where it won widespread and popular support.

5
Political protest

Between 1780 and 1840 methods and types of popular political protest underwent enormous changes and developments. The period begins with the Gordon Riots in which the London crowd displayed little independent political thought and awareness and ends with the first major independent working-class movement the world has ever seen – Chartism. Those historians inclined to interpret these developments as progressive and modernising would be overlooking certain complexities and subtleties. Violent mob-like actions were still evident in the 1830s as indeed were manifestations of the vital but secret insurrectionary tradition that dated back to the 1790s. Indeed Chartism can trace its heritage back to the many reformist and radical traditions, not least the 'mass platform' built up by Hunt and others after 1815. It would be true, however, to observe that the English masses increasingly utilised new political techniques and actions, which suggested that the 'moral economy' and defence of custom were being replaced by more ambitious and ultimately more threatening activities which went beyond narrow economic demands. This would explain why the authorities became more apprehensive of popular protest. It possessed the language and the potential to be revolutionary.

The reactionary crowd

The term 'mob', indicating a mindless and irrational group, would seem at first sight to be an appropriate description for the London crowd which took control for nearly a week in June 1780. The Gordon Riots were not only the most violent episode of the eighteenth century in the capital, they have also never since been equalled in terms of people killed or executed in an episode of civil disorder. Likewise, the destruction of property was extensive, amounting to £100,000, which probably only twentieth-century bombing campaigns have surpassed.

Early studies of the riots, particularly by de Castro (1926) and the more popular account by Hibbert (1958), provide detailed narratives which describe the behaviour of the 'reckless', 'drunken and desperate' mobs in what has come to be regarded as the most complex and in some ways the most puzzling examples of civil commotion. The actual events surrounding their origins and the progress of the riots are not in dispute. All historians are agreed that Lord George Gordon, leader of the Protestant Association, attempted to petition Parliament in order to win a repeal of the 1778 Catholic Relief Act which had granted Roman Catholics a limited number of civil liberties. To further his cause, he adopted the traditional method of pressurising Parliament by orchestrating a mass lobby of 60,000 'of the better sort of tradesmen' (Rudé 1974: 269) to persuade Parliament to accept his petition for repeal. At this early stage the crowd was well ordered and disciplined, but its mood undoubtedly changed in part due to Gordon's demagogy. In consequence, the selective destruction of Catholic chapels began and over the next few days further chapels, mass houses, homes of wealthy Catholics and magistrates, including Lord Mansfield, the lord chief justice, who had had the temerity to arrest rioters for the chapel incidents, were all singled out for destruction. Rudé, among others, has emphasised the discipline of the crowd, which was highly selective in what it destroyed and careful to burn the contents of selected targets in the streets for fear of damaging neighbouring property. This phase of the rioting was marked by 'licensed spontaneity' (E. P. Thompson 1968: 77) by which the crowd was not prevented from attacking Catholic property, and whose anti-Catholic and no-popery sentiments were actively applauded not only by Gordon but also by the City of London authorities and a significant number of MPs.

This 'licence to riot' was removed once the situation started to go out of control on Tuesday evening and 'Black Wednesday' when Bow Street police office and the prisons were attacked and their inmates (except one murderer) freed. The climax came with the destruction of a gin distillery which led to a huge explosion and scenes of drunken rioters. At this point eighty-one houses caught light, more prisons were attacked, the toll bridge on Blackfriars was plundered and demolished, and attempts were made to storm the Bank of England. The city authorities, stirred into action by these scenes of anarchy which even Gordon could not control, deployed 10,000 troops on the streets, who shot or arrested the mob into submission by Thursday evening. It has been estimated that 210 rioters were killed outright on the streets, a further 75 died in hospital and over 170 were wounded. In addition, 25 of the 450 arrested were executed (Rudé 1974: 275).

In the first major revision of the riots since the 1920s Rudé was able to draw on ample court material to investigate the composition of the crowd and the development of the riots. He played down the criminal element by pointing out that most prisoners released from the gaols were debtors rather than felons (Rudé 1974: 280), though we should not overlook the fact that looting did take place. The majority of those arrested were 'sober workmen' who were in employment and who certainly did not belong to the poorer sections of the labouring classes. Crucially for Rudé, the riots developed beyond their sectarian origins, becoming a 'groping desire to settle accounts with the rich' (ibid.: 289). This wider social protest, he maintained, can be discerned in the analysis of the victims. First, poor working-class Catholics, particularly the Irish who were never popular at the best of times, were not singled out by the mobs. Their neighbourhoods were left untouched (ibid.: 285). The victims, although Catholic or supporters of the Relief Act, were nearly all wealthy: gentlemen, merchants, publicans and a school teacher. Moreover, the institutions of authority such as the police office, the prisons and the bank were determinedly attacked. Thus, for Rudé, the London crowd with all its xenophobic, sectarian and racist baggage was developing its own rudimentary political awareness independent of the elite groups who had originally initiated them but who had lost both control and their nerve by Tuesday night. It was anti-Catholicism with a class hostility complexion. In pursuing this argument Rudé has overstated the crowd's orderliness and discipline; certainly the attacks by Wednesday show that they were out of control, which suggests the 'degeneration' model advanced by de Castro has something to commend it. More recently, Rogers has challenged Rudé's social protest interpretation whilst allowing for the fact that the crowd's victims were wealthier than the crowd were themselves. For most of its duration, Rogers has argued, the riot followed its pro-Protestant course in so far as the mob aimed to attack prominent Catholics who occupied important positions as teachers, shopkeepers and publicans within the community. However, in the final stages the riots changed direction and the targets became more specific, local and traditional, such as the attacks on the crimping and sponging houses and the much-hated Blackfriars toll-bridge (N. Rogers 1988: 31). The overall lessons from this dramatic episode were that political radicals were now understandably wary of the London crowd and that the movement for parliamentary reform was damaged, but, most important of all, that the memory of June 1780 was still very much alive when the news of the revolution in Paris came through in 1789.

The ingredients of reaction, nationalism, sectarianism and 'rent-a-mob' which had been all too evident during the Gordon Riots made an ugly reappearance in the 1790s once the full impact of the French Revolution began to reverberate on an already lively English political scene. Between 1791 and 1795 a number of plebeian riots, most notably in Birmingham, Nottingham and Manchester, occurred against dissenting middle-class reformers. These 'Church and King' Riots, as they became known, have not attracted the same historical attention as more politically progressive examples of working-class action for a number of reasons. First, the very reactionary and pro-conservative status quo attitude of such mobs do not fit comfortably with theses of emerging working-class consciousness. Second, many historians of the left have tended to see elements such as hired thuggery at work within these disturbances rather than genuine expressions of working-class patriotism. E. P. Thompson, who barely touched on such examples, noted that these loyalist mobs were hired hands largely under the control and direction of Tory magistrates who gave them 'licence' to riot (1968: 79–82). As such, these 'Church and King' mobs were not genuine displays of popular resentment against dissenters and reformers. It is hard to discover the true feelings and beliefs of the crowds because many of these mobs were indeed sponsored by the local magistracy and were consequently immune from arrest and prosecution. In the worst episode, the Priestley Riots of 1791 in Birmingham, when four dissenting meeting houses were destroyed and more than twenty-five homes attacked and damaged in five days of pandemonium and mayhem, four were found guilty and only two were hanged (R. B. Rose 1960). Rudé has, however, found within the Priestley Riots elements of 'latent class hostility' and social protest in which industrial workers and miners displayed 'a levelling instinct' against wealthy middle-class dissenters, many of whom were manufacturers and employers (Rudé 1964: 135–225).

In a more recent regional study of the North West, Booth (1983) has shown not only how much more widespread and frequent 'Church and King' Riots were but that they were not restricted to the main urban centres such as Manchester. In the twenty-five examples he discovered for the years 1791–5, many were small-scale affairs coinciding with local festivities or Tom Paine effigy burnings. Occasionally, they developed into very substantial affairs such as the 'Royston Races' in which 3,000–4,000 were involved. Although evidence of magisterial non-interference was apparent in many of these disturbances, Booth believes that the social resentment of the crowd should not be overstated since they attacked plebeian as well as middle-class reformers (ibid.: 305). Moreover, it should not be assumed that free drink was all that was required to hire a mob of anti-reformers. Loyalist propaganda was able to put forward persuasive arguments which contrasted the prosperity and the calm political status quo of Britain with the anarchy, disruption and economic collapse of France. Political radicals and the works of Tom Paine were consequently easy targets in these years of uncertainty and fear, which were made worse by the declaration of war with France in 1793.

The force of popular Toryism should not therefore be underestimated. It has had a long history down to the present day and has, at certain crucial times, overshadowed the popularity of more progressive working-class political movements. The crowd or mob, however, can be fickle in its loyalties, especially when prosperity turns to economic distress. As we have already seen, 1795 was a year of high prices and food riots and this led increasingly to a turnabout in popular sentiment. Where the magistracy had looked benignly on loyalist mobs in the early 1790s, they now mobilised soldiers against food rioters. Increasingly, many people began to view the authorities with distrust and sought solutions which had only a few years previously been regarded as 'un-English' or even revolutionary.

Reformist and insurrectionary traditions

The decade of the 1790s has been viewed as a watershed by a number of historians (Belchem 1981: 1) in terms of the foundations and growth of popular radicalism. Whilst they may differ in emphasis, they are all agreed that Tom Paine's *Rights of Man*, with its accessible language and clear political programme, the example and impact of the French Revolution, and governmental repressive legislation all combined in varying proportions to begin the long process of politicisation of the people culminating in the Reform struggle of the 1830s and, eventually, Chartism. During these years both the modes and the objectives of protest were gradually transformed. It is possible to see in the urbanising and industrialising North and Midlands a gradual decline of the 'traditional' and age-old food riot in defence of customary attitudes, and its replacement with overtly working-class movements that campaigned for a political voice and representation, trade unions and so forth. It would be erroneous, however, to view such changes as occurring in a neat linear manner: there were peaks and troughs of activity during the war years. Moreover, there also appeared contradictions.

It has already been seen how violent the loyal and pro-war crowd could be in the 'Church and King' Riots. This same crowd could attack radical shoemaker Thomas Hardy, founding member and secretary of the London Corresponding Society, and yet lionise him a few months later when he was acquitted in 1794. Whilst elements of popular conservatism were to remain throughout the war years, fluctuating in part with the fortunes of the British armed forces, a more resistant and influential current began to flow both in London and in the provinces. Anti-war feelings soon emerged in the anti-crimp house riots (Stevenson 1992: 208–12) in 1794–5 when press gangs and crimps were extremely active in London. (Crimps were a type of recruiting agent for the armed forces and the merchant navy, who either kidnapped men or lured them into 'crimp houses', which also served as brothels and taverns; the men would fall into debt and be forced to enlist and pay off their creditors with the advance wages they received.) In the provinces there was widespread rioting against the provision of balloting for the militia in Lincolnshire, East Anglia and in the far North in Cumberland (Charlesworth 1983: 127–30). These were spontaneous and largely traditional outbursts of popular anger against the pressures of war and owed nothing to the emerging radical movement in the capital.

Prior to the 1790s the reform movement was elitist, moderate and constitutional. Paine and his *Rights of Man*, which sold in excess of 200,000 copies between 1792 and 1795 and has been called 'the foundation text of the English working-class movement' (E. P. Thompson 1968: 99), educated skilled artisans in the politics of radical reform. However, his republicanism and his emphasis on natural rights as opposed to rights based on English history and constitutionalism were not particularly influential (Belchem 1981: 2). The popular radical movement which emerged among the so-called English Jacobins, such as the London Corresponding Society, was never very large or popular. The LCS membership, for example, probably peaked with a mere 3,000 members in the second half of 1795 (Emsley 1985a: 812). However, it did organise a number of mass meetings – the 'mass platform' in other words – and this was to become the defining tactic of the reform movement after 1816 (Stevenson 1992: 208). These earlier meetings at Copenhagen and St George's Fields proved enormously popular in 1795, when their calls for annual parliaments, universal manhood suffrage and an end to the war fell on attentive ears because of high food prices and the anti-war sentiment, which were merging to produce an increasingly discontented London populace. The LCS was emphatically against the use of violence and rioting but its tactic of holding mass meetings, each probably attended by in excess of 100,000, who heard impassioned demands for reform, no doubt contributed to rising tension in the capital. Whilst no direct link can be made, the authorities certainly made a connection between the LCS and the attack on the king in December 1795, which brought in repressive legislation banning seditious meetings and practices in the form of the Two Acts.

It is generally accepted that this legislation helped contribute to the demise of the radical reform of the corresponding society variety and aided the rise of what E. P. Thompson has called the 'secret revolutionary tradition' – a political underground movement that existed between the late 1790s and 1820, and which occasionally showed itself at crucial moments of revolutionary tension. In positing the existence of a revolutionary strand to English working-class history Thompson was challenging the traditional interpretations largely put forward by the Hammonds, who tended to argue for the existence of a moderate, constitutional and peaceful development of the working-class political movement. For Thompson, there was a more or less continuous revolutionary movement which can be traced through the United Englishmen and the United Irishmen, the Black Lamp, the Despard Conspiracy and Luddism to Pentrich in the post-war period (1968: 539).

The leading figure of this revolutionary strand at the turn of the century was Colonel Edward Despard. He is at first sight an unlikely revolutionary leader, coming as he did from an Irish landowning family. As a member of both the London Corresponding Society and United Britons, he appears to have plotted the revolutionary overthrow of the government. Like later conspirators (see below, 65–6), he believed that the taking of the Tower of London and the Bank of England would somehow set off a chain reaction of revolt in the capital. In the case of the Despard Conspiracy of 1802 there were, in addition, more serious plans laid by revolutionary groups. Evidence exists that indicates that the English underground movement had links with both France and Ireland. This may suggest that the Despard Conspiracy was a premature rising which was meant to have coincided with the French invasion of Britain and an Irish rebellion (Elliot 1977; Wells 1983). However, the seriousness of the threat posed by the conspiracy and the actual role played by Despard have been disputed by Elliot. She has argued that there was no Despard Conspiracy, but that a conspiracy did exist which was not of Despard's making (Elliot 1977: 61). The exact nature of the coup and the role played in it by Despard will never be known, as he remained silent during his trial for treason.

Also involved in this revolutionary coup was the Black Lamp of Lancashire and the West Riding of Yorkshire. Once again much of the detail of this shadowy revolutionary group is disputed, since the surviving evidence relating to the Black Lamp is thin, of questionable veracity and open to interpretation. Dinwiddy has criticised Thompson for his partial use of what little evidence there is and of also relying too much on an untrustworthy government agent who was later sacked. Whilst he concedes that Lancashire, rather than Yorkshire, may have been more militant, he feels that Thompson's emphasis on this revolutionary strand was 'nearer to myth' (1974: 123). Since then, further evidence and argument has tended to support Thompson's overall thesis of a revolutionary tradition. In Sheffield, a known revolutionary hotbed, personnel involved in the United Englishmen and the Despard Conspiracy have been identified, even though the conspiratorial grouping called the Black Lamp is now considered not to have existed (Baxter and Donnelly 1974: 124–32). The words 'Black Lamp' have probably been misread by the historian Aspinall and should in fact read 'Black Lump'. Even though a descriptive phrase has evolved into a conspiratorial organisation, this error has not, according to Baxter and Donnelly, called into question the existence of the revolutionary underground movement. Two important aspects appear to have emerged from the research: namely that elitist conspirators were able to attract and manipulate a substantial – just how substantial is impossible to estimate – group of workers, particularly in the North. Second, the tendency to view the moderate and revolutionary strands as separate may have been overstated. Militant elements within the London Corresponding Society along with Despard helped form the United Britons, a pattern which was repeated among the grass roots in Lancashire (Elliot 1977: 52). Depending on the pressure of the times it appears that individuals would move in and out of insurrectionary politics, which suggests that those historians who have regarded the United Britons as merely a crazed minority of fanatics could well be wrong (Booth 1986: 278). Although this 'physical' force strand of radicalism fell away for nearly a decade, it should not be dismissed lightly given the Luddite disturbances of 1811–12, and more importantly the Pentrich uprising of 1817, when the government spies reported meeting radicals who had been ready to rise with Despard in 1802 (Baxter and Donnelly 1974: 131). Moreover, in London the Despard tradition of insurrection was reactivated in 1816 by the so-called Revolutionary Party, which attempted to recruit working-class members (Parssinen 1972) and also to use the pacific mass meetings on Spa Fields to agitate and set off insurrection; one of the resulting disturbances was a very sorry affair organised by the Watsons, father and son London radicals. This occurred in December 1816 when an outdoor meeting was organised to mobilise the London crowd behind the idea of a national convention. Prior to the arrival of Henry Hunt, a young radical named Watson led a small breakaway group off into the city where they looted gunsmiths. Although a fairly minor affair, it had the effect of provoking the government into banning meetings of fifty or more persons and suspending *habeas corpus*. In 1820, another pathetic attempt at agitating the people into revolution was made by Thistlewood and others with their plan to assassinate the cabinet, in what has become known as the Cato Street Conspiracy. This episode belonged very much in the tradition of the revolutionary coup as espoused by Despard and the Watsons at Spa Fields. In the case of Cato Street, the name relates to the location where the conspirators were arrested. This conspiracy had been known to the government for two months through information provided by the *agent provocateur*, George Edwards. Although the plan looks desperate and unrealistic to our eyes, Thistlewood was well known to other more moderate radicals in London, who like him had to suffer the close attentions of government spies. However, with his execution more moderate tactics and methods of extra-parliamentary pressure prevailed (Stevenson 1992: 244–5; Prothero 1979: 116–31).

Before turning to the reform movement in more detail it is as well to consider the insurrectionary tradition in provincial England where, in some cases, the government believed that it had rather ominously merged with constitutionalist petitioning groups. A case in point is the March of the Blanketeers, in which peaceful protesters intent on marching to London with petitions were attacked and dispersed by the authorities who felt that revolutionary Spenceans were behind it (Stevenson 1992: 278; Bamford 1967: 29–33). As in other cases of insurrection it is difficult to decide where the truth lies because in this case much of the evidence was provided by *agents provocateurs* such as the notorious Oliver the Spy. In the Hammonds' opinion Oliver was the instigator of Pentrich; as a consequence they denied the existence of a genuine proletarian revolutionary element (Hammond and Hammond 1979: 278–307). But such an explanation ignores both the role of men like Thomas Bacon, a radical framework knitter, who was touring the Midlands and the North, and the links between Pentrich and the earlier Luddite disturbances. In Thompson's view, Oliver was an *agent provocateur* but one who was operating within a pre-existing revolutionary conspiracy that was widespread and not local as claimed by Thomis (Thomis and Holt 1977: 43–62). Moreover, Thompson has argued that Pentrich was historically significant because it was the first example of working-class insurrection which had no middle-class input (1968: 723–4). Its lasting significance was somewhat muted when compared with the so-called constitutionalist strand of radicalism.

The reform movement

Between the 1790s and 1815 popular grievances were undoubtedly politicised and more and more of the working classes came to view their solution as lying through parliamentary reform, which would in turn redress their economic grievances. This more moderate and popular strand of radicalism owed much to the charismatic leadership of individuals such as Burdett in London, William Cobbett the journalist and Henry Hunt as orator. Of the three, Burdett has been credited with keeping alive the spirit of parliamentary reform through the war years in London (Dinwiddy 1980) and even further afield. In terms of constitutional reform he was not, as a moderate, prepared to lend his support to more democratic variants of the reform movement, nor did he entirely trust the London crowd. Consequently, when peace with France came in 1815 Burdett was superseded by more radical champions like Hunt, Cartwright and Cobbett, who espoused universal manhood suffrage, but his overall contribution should not be underrated. The 'mass platform' of constitutional radicalism owes more to him than does the insurrectionary strand (ibid.: 20–30).

Burdett was essentially an elitist who was not prepared to utilise the masses. New methods and tactics of extra-parliamentary pressure politics came into existence after 1815, in what Belchem has called 'the mass platform', which became more influential in the North than in London. Henry Hunt, more than anyone else, became the 'champion of the unrepresented people' and it was his brand of radicalism which came to dominate even that of Cartwright's Hampden Clubs – reform clubs – originally founded in 1812. The clubs were intended to spread the constitutional and moderate message of reform to the working classes. Hunt's care in staying within the law and his emphasis on discipline at the mass open air meetings might suggest that Hunt was himself a moderate but nothing could be further from the truth. His biographer has called Hunt's tactics 'confrontational' politics (Belchem 1981, 1985) in which he had to be able to intimidate the government and yet stay within the law. He was in some ways walking a tight-rope between the threat of insurrection on the one side and the moderation of constitutional radicalism on the other. This was impossible to sustain for any length of time. It was, however, immensely successful and popular: the mass meetings were exciting and emotional occasions which did not attract unduly adverse publicity but yet simultaneously had to appear intimidating. Hunt and the other leading advocate of reform, the journalist and editor of the *Political Register*, William Cobbett, were able to redefine constitutionalism by arguing that the government and not the protesters were the traitors and that, this being the case, the people possessed the right to resist (Epstein 1989: 86; Belchem 1981: 11). The radicals also appropriated other symbols such as the 'cap of liberty'; they and their opponents agreed that such symbols had meaning and importance, though the two groups had precisely opposite interpretations. Such symbols had the same power as military colours and, during the Peterloo massacre, radicals did their best to defend the caps whilst the yeomanry and constables did their utmost to capture them (Epstein 1989: 99).

Closely related to these symbols was the prominence of women in the reform movement of 1818–19. Their presence, along with that of children, indicated the peaceful intent of the mass meetings, but their attendance also suggested political awareness and involvement. Women were now fully engaged in the movement, establishing their own associations, presenting addresses as at Blackburn (Epstein 1989: 101–7; Belchem 1981: 13) and voting at meetings. It was their presence, along with children and men, that not only added weight of numbers to the meeting at St Petersfield, Manchester in August 1819, but which gave it an essentially celebratory carnival atmosphere that was not particularly threatening. The name of Peterloo has entered the pantheon of English working-class history and is viewed as some kind of watershed, though in reality it was a bloody and spectacular defeat for the radical movement. Its infamy rests on the death of 11 people and the 400 injured, many of whom bore the cuts and scars of sabres wielded by the yeomanry who had been sent in to arrest Hunt on the platform. Such milestone events have attracted their own controversy, and Peterloo is no exception. Eyewitness accounts abound, since many non-partisan journalists were present, as indeed was Bamford the Lancashire radical (Bamford 1967: 148–58). The debate revolves around the issue of responsibility for the massacre. Read (1958), author of one of the best accounts, places the blame squarely on the incompetent local magistracy who, it must be said, had lived in an atmosphere of growing tension and fear of impending insurrection in the months leading up to the Peterloo meeting. Thompson, for his part, saw something approaching a government conspiracy at work in which Sidmouth, the home secretary, wanted a reckoning with popular radicalism. The longest, most detailed and, in some ways, least satisfactory interpretation has been put forward by Walmsley (1969) who, in disagreeing with other historians, has argued that no one was to blame. Of the three versions, Read's probably commands most respect since he was able to provide evidence of Sidmouth's order to the Manchester magistrates to go carefully and not intervene unless absolutely necessary. Moreover, he conclusively portrays the incompetence of the magistracy.

As with the Luddites, the debate on Peterloo is irresolvable, as Kirk's excellent review makes plain (1989). In many ways the obtuseness of the debate misses more important issues surrounding Peterloo, not least the failure of Hunt's tactics of 'forcible intimidation' (Belchem 1981: 14). The massed ranks of orderly and disciplined workers, rather than bringing the government to its knees, brought confusion to a movement whose leadership was not prepared to employ violence when all else had failed. For a brief while the grass roots of the movement were in insurrectionary mood, until the government clamped down with the infamous 'Six Acts' restricting the radical press and mass meetings. It remained only for a few foolhardy souls to gather on the Yorkshire moors in the spring of 1820 to remind the authorities that the insurrectionary underground tradition had not quite been extinguished (Belchem 1996: 49). The real gainers at Peterloo were the Whigs, since the massacre evoked from sections of the middle class widespread sympathy for the need for reform, and this was going to become evident at the end of the 1820s. In the meantime, Liverpool's government brought further opprobrium upon itself with the strange Queen Caroline affair of 1820, which was more reminiscent of eighteenth-century London crowd action than the more progressive but temporarily moribund reform movement (Stevenson 1977a: 117–48). This episode arose out of George IV's attempt to divorce his estranged wife, Caroline of Brunswick, who returned to England in 1820 when he became king. Both the radical press, especially the influential *Political Register*, and the London populace took up support for her cause. Her role as a victim of the establishment gave reformers and radicals the opportunity to criticise the Tory government. Her campaign to be made queen faded away in early 1821 when she accepted a pension, and popular support for her was notably absent when she attempted to gain admittance to the king's coronation at Westminster Abbey in April that year. Ironically, the main displays of support and emotion by the London crowd were reserved for her funeral procession in the summer of 1821. By barricading certain streets, the crowds were able to block the government's proposed funeral route and force the queen's coffin to travel through the city of London.

Government repression and an improving economy generally made the 1820s a quiet decade when compared with what had gone before and what was to come after. However, the repeal of the Combination Acts in 1824, the 1826 economic downturn and single issues such as Catholic emancipation ensured that popular agitation was never long out of the news. The year 1830 marked the start of a two-year Reform Crisis, the seriousness of which has been debated by historians ever since. The Reform Bill crisis represented the conjunction of 'high' politics and popular extra-parliamentary pressure. Discerning whether the latter was more important than the former is, like the revolution question, a contested one. The standard works by Brock (1973), Cannon (1973) and Hamburger (1963), for example, all consider such issues. Generally speaking, historians would argue that public pressure and demand were not as influential at bringing about reform as some earlier historians implied. The latter were in some cases relying on the rather partial accounts of reformers like Francis Place who clearly had a desire to emphasise his own role in the process. More decisive were the positions and actions taken up by the Whigs and Tories during these years, not least during the 'Days of May' in 1832, when Place claimed armed resistance would have broken out had reform not taken place (Cannon 1973: 239).

Such an outcome may well have been fanciful in that radical working-class groups such as the National Union of the Working Classes were weak and divided (Rowe 1977: 167–8). This should not deny them a role, nor should we overlook some admittedly tense moments and situations for the ruling elite. The whole background to the first Reform Bill was one of crisis, there being revolutions in Europe, Captain Swing Riots in the rural shires and movements for national and general unions led by Doherty. Such pressures ensured that the new Whig government was extremely apprehensive of a possible revolution, especially if the middle and working classes allied together in the way they had briefly in Paris and Brussels in 1830. The newly established Political Unions would appear to have offered that possibility but regional differences in terms of membership and leadership suggest that the radical reform movement was never unified (Stevenson 1992: 297).

Although there were violent incidents related to reform from the summer of 1830, mass protest broke out only when the House of Lords rejected the second bill in October 1831. The reaction ranged from restrained anger in the capital where the Duke of Wellington's windows were broken, to the more dramatic and unrestrained rioting in Derby, Nottingham and above all Bristol, which Rudé has termed 'the last great urban riot in English history' (1988: 176). Echoes of the Gordon Riots can be found in this latter incident, not just the enormous scale of damage done to property, but also in the inactivity of the law enforcement agencies in repressing the rioting and the newspaper reports, and in eyewitness accounts that criminals and the very poor were responsible. In fact, those arrested were frequently in work and of previous good character (Harrison 1988: 286–314). The violence of the late autumn was more 'paroxysmal' (Palmer 1988: 389) in character than continuous, nor did it appear to be building up to some terrible crescendo. Consequently, nothing quite like Bristol was experienced again during the Reform Crisis. Working-class opinion was deeply divided on the bill; in London and particularly Birmingham, social classes collaborated under the leadership of Attwood (Rowe 1977; Wright 1988: 91–4). This perhaps reflects the close social ties between master and men in the metal workshops (Rowe 1977), although this has been questioned by more recent research (Behagg 1979). In such circumstances the middle-class leadership was using the working classes as a threat in the same way as the loyalists had given plebeian groups licence to riot in the 1790s, or what Belchem has memorably called a 'middle-class version of collective bargaining by riot' (1996: 61). In the North, the working classes, were not, however, at the beck and call of the middle-class leadership. Here, the Political Unions were proletarian in character, again reflecting the vast social distance between classes and economic developments which had taken place in Manchester and other industrial centres (Dinwiddy 1986: 66). The reform movement was thus divided in the months leading up to successful passage of the bill through Parliament in 1832, by which time popular disillusionment was already being channelled into other movements such as Owenism, trade unionism and the Factory Movement, all of which indicated a deep chasm between the middle classes and the increasingly radical and independent working classes. This disillusionment was to prove crucial to Chartism, with its espousal of radical democratic reform.

Post-1832

The Reform Crisis had introduced mass popular politics on a national scale and the experiences gained in these years were put to further use when the Whigs introduced the Poor Law Amendment Act in 1834. Popular agitation against its implementation has, it has been argued, traditionally been underemphasised or has been at best viewed as an adjunct to the more influential and long-lasting movements such as the Ten-Hour Movement or Chartism (Ward 1962; Gray 1996). In the former, the Northern and industrial towns in the West Riding and Lancashire had been campaigning since the beginning of the decade for factory reform and 'short-time' under the leadership of Oastler and Sadler. As with the Reform Crisis, temporary alliances were formed between textile operatives and, in this case, Tory middle classes, who established a network of committees, mostly proletarian in composition in Lancashire, which attempted to pressurise the government into further reforms (Ward 1962). But the most important single issue of the mid-1830s concerned the implementation of the New Poor Law which, as has been shown, had sparked off riots in the rural South. The act itself passed with little reaction from Northern radicals who assumed that the legislation was more relevant to the pauperised villages of rural England which, unlike many Northern parishes, had failed to initiate their own local cost-cutting reforms. When the Northern protest came, it was 'violent and passionate' (M. E. Rose 1966: 70) but short-lived, being restricted to the years 1837–9. Geographically, the anti-New Poor Law movement was not experienced in all manufacturing and industrial areas, as the North East and the former Luddite centres of the Midlands were quiescent. It was concentrated, predictably, in the textile centres of the West Riding and East Lancashire where it would seem that the movement owed a considerable debt to the Factory Movement in terms of tactics, organisation and personnel. This explains why the Northern agitation was so much more sustained than in the South (Edsall 1971; see above, 24–6).

Historians have now recognised the importance of the anti-Poor Law movement in its own right. Both Rose and Edsall have traced its history whilst more recently Knott (1986) has added a number of additional details. These accounts stress the anger, horror and fears of the working classes who again worked in alliance with middle-class Tories, traditionalists and paternalists in combating the actual implementation of the act from 1836 when the assistant commissioners began arriving in the industrial Northern towns. This co-incided with a substantial though short-lived trade depression in the textile sector, and it soon became obvious that the New Poor Law would not be able to administer the workhouse test to the unemployed. Anger at the reforms came from two directions: first, the intended centralisation under the Poor Law Commission was particularly loathed by local vestries and relieving officers, who often prided themselves on their careful administering of relief. Second, the popular protest which was expressed in the language of lost rights and religion – the New Poor Law being 'the will of lucifer' (M. E. Rose 1966: 77) – hinged around the dreaded workhouse or bastille and the largely exaggerated rumours and stories then circulating of the cruelties of the system in Southern England. Physical violence, mass demonstrations and riots occurred in Bradford, Huddersfield and Todmorden, among other places where the anti-Poor Law movement used working people as the shock troops to disrupt the implementation of the New Poor Law. Once again, the threat of mass violence – the 'language of menace' tactic – proved successful in forcing the Poor Law Commission to abandon implementation of the new orders. The very success of the movement led to its downfall: as the workhouse test was not implemented, the horror stories never came to pass. Moreover, through the pages of the *Northern Star* in 1837, Fergus O'Connor played a leading role not only in providing propaganda against the New Poor Law but also in stirring up anti-middle-class attitudes among proletarian activists. By late 1838, therefore, the anti-New Poor Law movement had been swallowed up in the North by the more radical and all-encompassing Chartist movement (Edsall 1971: 167–86), which had among its many political objectives the promised repeal of the New Poor Law. Chartism, which is deserving of its own separate study (Brown 1998; Royle 1996; Walton 1999), represented the culmination of the many movements which have been outlined here: namely parliamentary reform, trade unionism, factory reform and anti-New Poor Law sentiment. The Chartists' tactics, too, owed a considerable debt to the experiences of the years since 1815, not least the distrust of allying with the middle classes, but more importantly their adoption of the 'language of menace'. Even the insurrectionary tradition, which can be traced back to the turn of the century, emerges in the failed uprising of 1839. Chartism was both the culmination of what had gone before and also the first truly independent working-class movement.

6
Policing protest

In recent years historians have increasingly investigated the obverse side of the riot or 'contentious gathering', namely the role, behaviour and response of the authorities. In many respects we have been able to interpret popular gatherings as historical events precisely because the authorities had chosen to intervene in order to placate or suppress the crowd. Moreover, their intervention generally led to either disorder or increased disorder as the very presence of law enforcement agencies could in themselves become an issue of dispute for the crowd. This is especially true during this period when the unofficial and unspoken rules of popular demonstrations, as evinced in food riots, for example, came to be regarded as unacceptable, dangerous and potentially revolutionary by the beleaguered authorities at both central and local government levels.

How authority was exercised in the eighteenth century varied from one region to another, which makes generalisation difficult. However, it is possible to identify an urban–rural dichotomy in which law enforcement became more repressive and less tolerant in towns and cities earlier than in the countryside. But even in the towns the largely amateur magistracy (only the very largest cities had stipendiaries by 1820) had to achieve a delicate balance between law enforcement and social peace, since the former could well upset the latter. In a country which prided itself on not possessing a standing army and having only a rudimentary parish constable system, the wonder is why there was so little disorder. Rioting, as has been shown, was rarely random in its targets nor was it an explosion of anarchic violence; rather it was a selective and limited tactic of redress or negotiation. Such a process suggests that the populace accepted to a large extent 'the legitimacy of the rule of law'

(Brewer and Styles 1983: 11–20) and the elites whose role it was to rule. The crowd's challenge was therefore set within tightly defined parameters, which were understood by both sides in the dispute.

This was especially the case in provincial England where the local authorities were relatively powerless in terms of the law enforcement weaponry which they could bring to bear on the populace in times of stress. The social peace was often achieved through maintaining the social cohesiveness of the communities and their acceptance of the notions of 'reciprocal obligations' (Dunkley 1979: 371) and *noblesse oblige*. Hay, in one of the most elegant and sophisticated essays on this theme, has argued that a tiny ruling elite was able to maintain its position through control and manipulation of an increasingly 'bloody code', in which there were over 200 capital statutes by 1800 but the elite resorted to them with decreasing frequency (Hay 1975). This is not a classic marxist analysis of naked class power and repression in so far as Hay (ibid.) and E. P. Thompson (1975b: 258–69) have both argued that the ruling class were themselves subject to this law. As important was their ability to dispense justice in a flexible manner by deciding when and how harshly to punish recalcitrant members of their communities. The ruling elite possessed the prerogative of mercy and could evoke 'gratitude as well as fear in the maintenance of deference' (Hay 1975: 41). Time and again during this period the authorities often executed just one or two rioters *pour décourager les autres* whilst being reasonably lenient on the remaining defendants. The latter action thus evoked the gratitude of the defendants, their relatives and the community at large. As a consequence, the social standing and authority of the local gentry were enhanced. Moreover, the twin forces of terror and mercy enabled them to rule without recourse to either a standing army or a professional police force. This persuasive and seminal argument has not gone unchallenged (Langbein 1983), but critics have generally disputed only some of the technical detail of the trial process. More profoundly, Hay's unduly gentry-centred analysis has underestimated the role and importance of the 'middling groups' in society, such as shopkeepers and farmers (King 1984). These people played a much more prominent role in the criminal justice system as prosecutors and jurymen than did the local gentry. This was even more evident in London and other large towns where the victims of crime were small property owners and the juries composed of shopkeepers. Both the prosecutors and the jurymen occupied key positions in the decision-making process of the criminal justice system. They could determine whether defendants ran the risk of execution by deciding on what charge they were tried (ibid.).

In the context of studies on popular disorder, Hay's analysis is never applied to London and, as the eighteenth century developed, it applies less and less to those regions undergoing rapid industrialisation, population growth and urbanisation. Paternalism and the bonds of deference in these urban communities were no longer applicable, and the character and the level of popular disorder which were becoming evident by the end of the century are symptomatic of a breakdown in community social relations. Confrontation, it has been argued by Bohstedt, became increasingly more violent and disorderly in urban areas such as Manchester, although this should not be overstated (Charlesworth 1993). As yet, no interpretative overview of the kind Hay has provided for the eighteenth century exists for the nineteenth. The nearest and most thought-provoking has been Gatrell's 'Crime, Authority and the Policeman State' (1990) which attempts, in part, to take up the analysis where Hay's earlier system of control has broken down.

Popular disturbances, as we have seen, were not static phenomena. The same could also be said of the authorities' definitions of orderly behaviour. How threatening the crowd was and whether it required policing were questions which came to occupy the minds of those in authority with increasing frequency by the beginning of the nineteenth century. Why this should be the case is not difficult to understand, although the significance of the various factors has been differentially emphasised by historians. In short, crowds and the working-class masses came to be perceived as potentially threatening, and their public gatherings were tolerated less and less. This tendency towards increasing intolerance was fed by socio-economic changes and demographic growth; in the latter case, a cause for concern was the increasing concentration of working people in the towns, not least London where one in ten Englishmen lived at the end of the eighteenth century. The organic face-to-face social relations in traditional society ceased to exist in the new urban environment, giving rise to feelings of insecurity and fear among the ruling class. Where social distance existed, the very presence of the masses was seen as threatening, and they were seemingly beyond the control of the authorities with their limited law enforcement forces. The government's new approach to collecting statistical criminal data from 1810 served only to feed these fears even more, since the figures suggested that crime was rapidly outstripping the rise in population. Fear of the masses would have undoubtedly existed even if the French Revolution had not occurred. The events across the Channel not only acted as an acute warning to the ruling elite, they also supported a growing belief that popular protest was potentially revolutionary and subversive, especially as Britain was at war for a generation. The fear and the need for order were not simply products of foreign events, since the Gordon Riots are frequently viewed by historians as some kind of turning point which highlighted the fragility of the status quo and the power of the 'mob' in the absence of effective law enforcement agencies in the capital.

Law enforcement

What was at the disposal of the magistracy, who were effectively the crucial controlling authority for most of England over much of the period? The list of bodies is impressively long and expanded further during the war: parish constables, special constables, the militia, yeomanry, Chelsea out-pensioners, self-help associations, the coastguard service and, when all else failed, the regular army (Mather 1959). Major conurbations, especially London, already possessed a relatively effective, efficient and substantial police before Peel's Metropolitan police reform of 1829 (Paley 1989: 115–16). Impressive as this list seems, historians have concluded that England was 'an underpoliced society' (Eastwood 1994: 191). When policing of riots was required, it was 'a hit or miss affair' (Emsley 1985a: 822) partly because public disorder was tolerated to a limited extent, but more importantly because repression was constrained by the weakness of the law enforcement agencies. Pragmatism and realism frequently dictated policing methods and techniques, especially in the eighteenth century. The ubiquitous parish constable found in every parish prior to the nineteenth-century police reforms has attracted surprisingly little historical attention, but that which has been forthcoming has been highly critical of the system's policing effectiveness. This universal condemnation stems in part from Chadwick's damning indictment of this institution in the 1839 Rural Constabulary Report (Storch 1989) and from evidence of their inactivity and inertia at times of disorder. These unpaid, annually elected parish officers belonged to the communities in which they served and consequently they could sympathise with the collective anger or at least collaborate with the crowd (Bohstedt 1983: 38–9) and lend the disturbance some 'official' backing. Many officers were middle or lower middle class in social origin and thus did not always identify with the popular disturbances, especially where private property was being damaged, as in the Swing Riots. Their vulnerability to revenge attacks meant that discretion was for many the better part of valour, although it has to be noted that one of the very few persons to be killed by a crowd was a Birmingham constable during the Priestley Riots of 1791 (Babington 1990: 35). Until more research is conducted on the constables, it would be unwise to dismiss them as cowardly and useless, since they may have played an important and influential mediating role between the magistrates and the rioters.

Better documentation exists on the effectiveness of special constables who were sworn in at times of local crisis. Their numbers could be impressively large – over 1,000 were sworn in when Sir Francis Burdett was released from gaol in 1810 (Palmer 1988: 148). Being property owners and middle-class, specials were equally as vulnerable as the parish constables to revenge attacks in rural areas (Archer 1990: 103) during the Swing Riots and the anti-Poor Law disturbances. In the more impersonal setting of the towns, where specials were not as susceptible to intimidation, their effectiveness was limited by the fact that they were not stationed where they were most needed in the Luddite disturbances, for example. In the districts of Nottingham with 600 men on street patrol and in Salford with one-tenth of its male population sworn in, the specials needed to be out in the industrial villages and not in the cities (Palmer 1988: 180; Darvall 1969: 252–3). However, in the extreme panic of the Gordon Riots and to a lesser extent Swing, private citizens organised themselves into patrol associations; they often bore arms which, had they had recourse to use, would have created legal complications (Palmer 1988: 86–7). Similar private armies of farming tenants, amounting almost to vigilante groups (Hobsbawm and

Rudé 1973: 217) were led around the countryside of Southern England on manhunts. For Palmer (1988: 148), the existence and willingness of private citizens to step in and police their own communities were an important factor in slowing down the introduction of professional policing.

Amateur policing was frequently overwhelmed and underarmed, especially during the war years when the authorities felt vulnerable to civilian disturbances. New quasi-military bodies either expanded or emerged, not least the militia, the volunteer movement and, most infamously, the yeomanry. Although recruited to fight French invasion, they became the foremost peace-keeping forces in both Britain and Ireland. The English militia averaged around 50,000–80,000 in numbers for most of the war, whereas the yeomanry, which was established in 1794, reached 25,000 by 1803 (Palmer 1988: 160). So far as the authorities were concerned, the foot soldiers of the militia and the volunteer movement shared the same defects, of being ineffective and even mutinous in times of civil strife because they sympathised with protesters (Radzinowicz 1968: 112). At Branscomb and Seaton, Devon, volunteers took a leading role in the price-fixing riots of 1800. Bohstedt has further claimed that they were called upon to repress riots on just five occasions and yet they joined the side of rioters in sixteen food riots in 1795 (1983: 56, 250 n. 112). Not only does this suggest that they were imbued with the same beliefs as the rioting crowd, it also confirms that they drew a distinction between their role as a quasi-military force raised to defend the nation, which they would happily comply with, and their role as a domestic police peace-keeping force, which they often found abhorrent.

The most successful civilian forces of all, from a policing standpoint, were the yeomanry. Established as a cavalry force, they were largely composed of landowners, farmers and small businessmen, and consequently rarely sympathised with either the demands of the crowd or their methods of redress (Radzinowicz 1968: 112–13). They were deployed against most types of crowd action ranging from the Luddites to political radical meetings, Swing and the Poor Law riots of the 1830s. Their presence tended more often than not to exacerbate tense, but otherwise calm, situations because of their class hatred for the demonstrators and their enthusiasm for restoring 'order'. Nowhere is this so evident as in the Peterloo Massacre of

1819. Their precise role and responsibility in triggering off the killing of eleven people was much disputed at the time by eyewitnesses both for and against the Manchester and Salford Yeomanry Corps and has since been fiercely debated by historians (see above, 68–9). On the one hand E. P. Thompson (1968) and Kirk (1989) have defended the radicals' version of events, whilst Babington (1990) and most especially Walmsley (1969) take the side of the hapless magistrates and the panicky yeomanry. A third 'commonsense' and widely respected interpretation put forward by Read (1958) lays the blame on the local magistracy, but absolves Sidmouth, the home secretary, who urged the Manchester authorities 'to abstain from any endeavour to disperse the mob, unless they should proceed to acts of felony or riot' (Palmer 1988: 187). To Walmsley, the magistrates and yeomanry confronted by a crowd of between 60,000 and 150,000 – the size of the meeting is disputed – of revolutionary intent had to defend themselves when attacked by radical militants. Regular soldiers who were called in to rescue the beleaguered yeomanry, according to accounts provided by both Hunt and Sidmouth, displayed discipline and comparative moderation to the extent that not a single death by sabre was apportioned to them. However, their Hussars' presence undoubtedly contributed to the further panic and crush of the masses; there were 560 reported wounded, 140 from sabre cuts.

Whilst the yeomanry continued to be called out during rural rioting, as in 1822 (Muskett 1984) and Swing, the government tended to rely increasingly on the regular army, which had long performed this policing role (Hayter 1978). The notion of a standing army was anathema to all Englishmen but their country came, at times, to resemble a military state responding to foreign war and internal rebellion and disorder in both England and Ireland. It has been estimated that half of the ninety-six permanent barracks in England between 1660 and 1847 were built between 1792 and 1815 (Palmer 1988: 160; Emsley 1983: 17–18), many of them in the newly industrialising towns of the North and Midlands which, during the Luddite disturbances, required a military force greater in number than that used by Wellington in the Peninsula War.

The position of the military when requested to act 'in aid of the civil power' has been well documented (Radzinowicz 1968: 115–23). Many uncertainties, ambiguities and legal complexities served to make the army's policing function extremely hard to perform. The Riot Act of 1715, for example, was one of the chief problems. This act has been described by Vogler (1991) as 'a law to abolish law' because it allowed for the use of force and the suspension of normal laws, although Radzinowicz has observed that martial law was not known in English law. This harsh measure defined a riotous assembly as consisting of twelve or more persons who, after one hour of the reading of the Riot Act, became felons who could be dispersed by the military. More often than not crowds did disperse and force was not required, which suggests that the one-hour breathing space between the reading and the army moving in allowed tempers to cool and the people to make their protest in the knowledge that nothing would happen to them. In these circumstances the act became part of the theatre of protest. The one-hour gap created confusion, it seems, for military commanders who thought the proclamation had to be read out and that a magistrate had to be present at the scene of the disorder before they could order their troops in to disperse the crowd. This uncertainty was based on the fact that these soldiers were, as General Napier pointed out, liable to both civil and military law. Under the former they could be tried for murder if death resulted from their actions; under the latter they could be court martialled if they had shown insufficient resolve. The magistracy likewise could be liable to prosecution if it was felt that they had been slow to act or had used excessive force in controlling crowds. Indecision and the refusal of justices of the peace to read the Riot Act during the Gordon Riots contributed to the escalation of the troubles. Order was restored in this instance only when the army were given permission to do as they pleased without a magistrate being required to be present. However, throughout the 1790s military officers continually sought clarification from the Home Office (Emsley 1983: 13–15) on their policing role and on their relationship with the civil authorities, whom many officers found timid and unhelpful.

The army were deployed during not only all the major outbreaks of trouble but also during smaller and more localised disturbances such as Queen Caroline's funeral and the Battle of Bosenden Wood. Were they effective in restoring order without causing undue bloodshed? Rudé, among others, has argued that military violence was greater in the eighteenth century when, for example, 285 were shot dead in the London streets in 1780, and a further 17 shot dead and over 50 wounded in the Bristol tollgate riots of 1793. Such heavy casualties were not, it is claimed, repeated in the nineteenth century, although the assertion that bloodshed was 'rare' in confrontations between the army and rioting crowds is probably overstating matters (Rudé 1973: 17–18). It has been estimated that only thirteen Luddite rioters were killed – twelve during the Bristol Reform riots of 1831 – and most dramatically nine killed in the battle of Bosenden Wood of 1838. The Chartist Newport Rising of 1839 with twenty dead represents the final bloodbath. That more were not killed in these and other disturbances is indicative of both the army's and the crowd's self-control and discipline. The former were, after all, untrained in policing civil disorders and armed with muskets, bayonets and sabres which were inappropriate for limited crowd-control measures. When they resorted to muskets, they generally shot over the heads of the crowd, but even this proved fatal in Rochdale when, in 1795, two onlookers were killed by the descending bullets (Emsley 1983: 16). Senior officers disliked their policing function and found their position subordinate to the magistracy humiliating and confusing. Their inappropriate weaponry and their role made them unpopular with the entire civilian population, from those whom they were policing to the local authorities who found the presence of troops in their localities unsettling and disruptive. All these shortcomings, which had been apparent to some since 1780, were all too evident to the legislature in the 1820s.

The 'new' police

Research on the history of policing has expanded enormously in recent years and has given rise to debates concerning its true purpose, the popularity of the police with the public and the motives behind their formation. This last question has some relevance to the theme of popular protest. Were the police formed primarily to combat rising crime or to restore public order in the face of a growing threat from the urban masses? Peel, the architect of the 1829 Metropolitan Police Act, argued in Parliament the necessity of fighting rising crime, which the existing policing bodies were incapable of doing (D. Taylor 1997: 14; Emsley 1991: 24). Historians are less inclined to accept Peel's stated position for a variety of reasons, not least because no one was or is sure whether the crime rate was rising. Moreover, Peel's exaggerated criticisms of 'old' policing groups, which Chadwick endorsed in the 1830s, is untenable given the findings of recent research by Paley (1989). It is more than likely that his experience of Irish police reform, which was crucially related to civil disorder, coloured his thinking, especially as popular radicalism possessed dangerously widespread appeal (Palmer 1988: 289). The origins of the 'new' police, it has been concluded, were 'fundamentally political' (Miller 1977: 8–10). Attempting to separate the need to combat rising crime (or the perception of such) and the fear of civil disorder may be unrealistic and artificial since the two were closely related elements of the same problem, namely the perceived growing moral decay of, and the necessity to control, the urban masses. Both crime and riot threatened society and the 'new' police were established to combat both. This common interpretative model, in which the police are introduced to combat identified problems, has rather intriguingly been challenged and the equation – disorder equals policing – revised. Both Silver (1967) and Paley (1989: 96–7) have suggested that perhaps 'rising standards of order' led to rising public expectation of good order and an increasing intolerance of criminality, violence and riotous protest (Silver 1967: 2–4). In the first years of its existence the Metropolitan force expended most of its energy on riot and crowd control (Radzinowicz 1968: 177–83) to such an extent that these have been termed their 'oldest' skills. The police made their first recorded massed baton charge, with the aid of the humble truncheon, during the reform riots of 9 November 1830. This successful tactic, invented ironically enough by the radical Francis Place, was considered superior to the methods used by armed soldiers, not least because the police had one hand free to grab rioters whilst the other, gripping a truncheon, could strike out: 'the thump of wood on a swede turnip' as Emsley's article so memorably put it (1985b). So successful were the police in the capital that the army were not called out throughout the Reform Crisis. The provinces, on the other hand, still had recourse to the overkill tactics of the military, particularly during the reform riots at Derby, Nottingham and Bristol, where extensive civilian casualties occurred.

The threats posed by public disorder rather than the fears generated by crime undoubtedly contributed to the 1835 Borough Police Act and the permissive 1839 County Police Act. The disturbances surrounding the implementation of the New Poor Law and Chartism led to a heavy demand for Metropolitan policemen to serve in the provinces, often with considerable success. Their effectiveness as a 'national riot squad' (Emsley 1985b: 128–9) helped break down lingering prejudices against policing in the provinces. One should, however, be cautious in attempting to correlate the establishment of county police forces in 1839–40 with popular protest. Storch, for example, found that, of the twenty-two Swing-affected counties, only twelve had established forces by 1842. Some of the worst affected Swing counties like Kent, Surrey and Berkshire rejected the 1839 legislation (Storch 1989: 250). A similar lack of correlation can be found with those counties which experienced anti-Poor Law disturbances. One may be able to conclude that such disturbances did affect attitudes to policing and almost certainly led, in some cases, to experimentation in policing prior to 1839. In counties as diverse as Norfolk and Lancashire, the realisation that the paternalistically structured society, with its mutual obligations and duties, was a thing of the past – the new Poor Law confirmed as much – meant that new policing methods were required to restore order. In conclusion, it should be noted that the introduction of the 'new' police was itself a cause of rioting and disturbance. Public acceptance of these 'blue bottles' could take many years (Storch 1975).

The law

Physical repression at the hands of the authorities was only one of a number of options available to the state. The law, both statute and common, and its potentially fatal outcome through the 'bloody code' were designed to keep the people in awe and obedient. The Riot Act was, as we have seen, frequently read to prevent freedom of assembly and it enabled summary execution if necessary. In addition, the common law on riot could be used by justices of the peace for groups as small as three persons, but this carried a relatively light sentence. And for much of rural England most of the clauses of the

1723 Black Act were still operative until the 1830s and used for arson, animal maiming and the sending of threatening letters (E. P. Thompson 1975b).

The extreme political and social tensions of this period generated an unprecedented legal response in the form of repressive statute laws aimed at the labouring classes. Between 1793 and 1820, more than sixty acts directed at working-class collective action were passed by Parliament, making this one of the most repressive periods in the nation's history. Did such governmental activity amount to, in the words of Place, 'a reign of terror' (cited in Hone 1977: 88) in the 1790s and beyond, and was this legislation effective in stemming popular hostility? The final six years of the eighteenth century appear to have been the most reactionary: the Habeas Corpus Act was suspended, and the Two Acts relating to treasonable and seditious practices and assemblies and the Combination Acts were passed. Virtually all working-class political and collective activity was banned (Emsley 1985a; Hone 1977: 79–81; Munger 1981: 117).

The government was partially successful in forcing radical societies into decline but Emsley has argued that this 'terror' has been exaggerated by Thompson and others. Comparing the panics surrounding the Jacobites earlier in the century, he found the prosecution of 200 radicals distinctly unimpressive (Emsley 1985a: 822). Similarly, the Combination Acts appear not to have closed down trade union activity, but it should be emphasised that these laws existed in the same way as did the 1797 Administering Unlawful Oaths Act and could be resorted to whenever the government required an example to be made. The Tolpuddle Martyrs certainly found this to be the case, as did Luddites prosecuted under the Combination Acts. The legal repression continued into the first two decades of the nineteenth century in two waves, the first covering the Luddite years when frame breaking was made a capital offence, and then between 1817 and 1820 when political reform and Peterloo gave rise to the 'Six Acts' which extended earlier legislation, especially stamp duty on periodicals, thus affecting adversely working-class newspapers.

Legal repression was probably at its most effective during trials after periods of collective disturbance. At first sight this may seem unlikely, as the numbers actually prosecuted for all forms of protest crime, from rioting to arson, were relatively insignificant when compared with more mundane forms of criminality such as theft. George Rudé, in a study covering the period 1825–74, found that protest crime amounted to only 5 per cent of all indictable crime. The most troubled year was 1831 when protest accounted for 8.5 per cent (1973: 10–11). But the numbers ending up in court represented the tiniest fraction of those who had actually taken part. The authorities, who were usually in a position to arrest only one or two 'ringleaders', tended also to release rioters without pressing charges, preferring instead to hold on to a small number either by way of 'hostage' taking in order to buy peace, or to prosecute and punish. Few food rioters were hanged (Wells 1988: 280), whereas twenty-five Gordon Rioters, thirty-six Luddites between 1812 and 1817, three involved in the Pentrich uprising, five Cato Street conspirators and four Bristol rioters were publicly executed. The Swing Riots were harshly repressed, with nineteen executions. What can seem puzzling to modern eyes is the range of sentences meted out to defendants. Many who were found guilty of capital offences had their sentences reduced to transportation. Again Rudé provides interesting figures that suggest protesters accounted for just 1.5 per cent of all convicts from England, Wales and Scotland who were transported to Australia and Van Dieman's Land (Rudé 1973: 19; 1978: 64). Of these 850 arrests, 505 resulted from the Swing Riots, a further 50 from the Luddite episodes and 34 cases from Bristol in 1831. Three riotous events provided 70 per cent of those protesters transported. Most commonly, punishment could appear lenient and strangely inconsistent. After the Captain Swing Riots, for example, in which 60 per cent of the 1,976 prosecuted were convicted, 644 were imprisoned (Hobsbawm and Rudé 1973: 224). Yet this figure probably represents only the tip of the iceberg in terms of people initially arrested but who were subsequently let off with a stern reprimand from justices of the peace (Archer 1990: 91). This initial leniency had not stemmed the rioting. If anything, the troubles escalated. As a consequence, the government deployed special commissions in five Southern counties and they, more than anything else, were responsible for the judicial savagery.

In conclusion, it is possible to state that the authorities had enormous repressive powers at their disposal in the form of the law and, more tangibly, the military. But it could be argued that the government's repressive controls were limited, not least because law enforcement agencies were geographically unevenly distributed and lacking in numbers. Therefore the question could be asked: why did the people not riot more often? More subtle controlling mechanisms were available, most importantly the Poor Laws and the vast range of philanthropic provision that was made available in town and countryside such as soup kitchens (Bohstedt 1983: ch. 4; Wells 1988: ch. 17), fuel, bread and even allotments (Archer 1997). Whilst charity was an attempt at buying the social peace and restoring the status quo, one should not always deny or dismiss the humanitarian concerns of the donors, who could be genuinely activated by religious and moral principles, and who regarded human misery as an affront to civilisation. Certainly, charity could reinvigorate paternalistic ties but, again, the social control mechanisms and explanations so frequently utilised by historians in the 1970s (Donajgrodzki 1977) require more rigorous application (F. M. L. Thompson 1981). But even the law, in conjunction with the military and social control, cannot provide the final missing element in explaining the crowd's relatively law-abiding behaviour: that must go to the self-control of the English working classes.

7
A revolutionary challenge?

The question of how close England came to revolution has been addressed by most historians working on this period. There is a general consensus that these decades possessed a revolutionary potential and, furthermore, that the country came as close as it had ever been to revolution since the seventeenth century. The consensus breaks down, however, when these scholars come to identify the most revolutionary year. Wells has pointed to the war years, especially 1799–1801 (1989: 32), Darvall to the Luddite year of 1812 (1969), White to the post-war period of 1817–19 (1968), whilst for E. P. Thompson Britain was 'within an ace of revolution' between 1831 and 1832 (1968: 898). Between these revolutionary 'moments' were interspersed individual events which were insurrectionary in character but lacking mass popular support. The naval mutinies of 1797, the Despard Conspiracy, Pentrich and Grange Moor, and Cato Street, for example, were in retrospect rather feeble attempts that in some cases were exaggerated by contemporaries, not least government spies and *agents provocateurs*. Consequently, some historians – such as Dickinson, Dinwiddy, Thomis and Holt – have been distinctly unimpressed by the proximity of revolution. Even the more sceptical of them allow that 'an idea of revolution, elusive in time and space, shape and form' (Thomis and Holt 1977: 1) did exist but that some of the schemes were wildly impractical and represented the hopes and ambitions of but a tiny minority. This raises the problem of definition as to what is meant by the term 'revolution'. As Stevenson has emphasised (1992: 326–30), England did not experience a revolution between the 1790s and 1840 and it is virtually impossible to judge how close the nation came to one since historians would not necessarily be able to identify a

revolutionary situation. Popular direct action and mass mobilisation should not be confused with revolution or revolutionary
potential.

In fact, this period experienced a variety of potential revolutionary styles including the small coup based on the capital, mutiny,
foreign involvement, provincial uprisings and the class alliance
aimed at pressurising the government into submission. Of all the
types listed, the coup based in London appears the least propitious
to modern eyes but was favoured by conspirators on a number of
occasions. In the case of the Despard Conspiracy, the revolutionaries hoped to capture the Tower of London and the Bank of England. But this begs the question of what they would have done then.
Such a plan required foreign help, not least a French invasion and
perhaps a simultaneous Irish uprising, neither of which was forthcoming. No revolutionary situation existed in 1802; there was a
temporary peace with France, the food crisis was receding and
London was not Paris. Britain by this time was far more decen-
tralised than France and it was thus highly unlikely that a coup in
the capital would have triggered off revolt elsewhere. In fact, it has
been argued that the London crowd was less militant than their
urban and industrial counterparts in the Midlands and the North
and, as a consequence, offered less potential to would-be revolutionaries (Stevenson 1992: 223, 327). The Cato Street Conspiracy, with its intention of assassinating the Cabinet, also lies within
this coup tradition. Again, the hope of Thistlewood and the others
lay in the spontaneous revolt that such an audacious action would
spark off. The timing was wrong, but it has been suggested that this
episode was not quite as isolated as it seemed (Prothero 1979:
116–31; E. P. Thompson 1968: 692–6, 769–80). As with the Despard Conspiracy, there were hints of a wider plan which may have
appeared in the Scottish and Yorkshire risings (Stevenson 1992:
286–7; Donnelly and Baxter 1975: 419–20).

Far more threatening to the state were the naval mutinies of
1797, which may or may not belong to the same revolutionary
tradition as those mentioned above. But what is abundantly clear
was the fact that the events at Spithead and the Nore were far more
subversive and significant than any threat a hungry or angry crowd
could muster. Had some ships sailed off to the enemy in France,
then the course of not only British but world history might have

been altered. Moreover, it is perhaps unwise to attribute the mutinies solely to the appalling conditions and low pay experienced by crews, though these were precisely the issues at stake in the minds of the majority of the mutineers. There are additional factors which need to be considered and weighed, not least the presence of the London Corresponding Society, Paineite ideology and slogans, and the intriguing presence of 11,500 Irish sailors and 400 Irish marines (E. P. Thompson 1968: 183–5; Wells 1983: 79–109), some of whom were members of the United Irishmen. Whilst the politically conscious revolutionaries did not initiate these mutinies, the crisis was exacerbated by their presence. The revolutionary potential was diffused by a mixture of the government's 'sensible handling' (Gilmour 1992: 444) of Spithead, exemplary punishment and the volatility of the sailors themselves who, according to the 'Admiral of the Floating Republic' of the Nore, Richard Parker, were 'cowardly, selfish and ungrateful' (E. P. Thompson 1968: 183–4).

Almost as alarming as military treason was the prospect of nation-wide uprisings, particularly in the Midlands and the North where a republican and revolutionary brand of politics was taking root. However, one would hesitate to view such disturbances as popular even in the radical heartland of the North West and the West Riding. As in the case of the Navy, it was largely the presence of militant United Irishmen that provided an important subversive and insurrectionary element, although one should not discount the home-grown militancy of these manufacturing regions. The conjunction of further food shortages, repressive legislation, war and trade disruption brought, for Wells (1988), the revolutionary moment in 1799–1801, which dissolved with the armistice and peace with France.

The Luddite troubles, particularly in 1812, are, as we have seen, the subject of much dispute. As Darvall has pointed out (1969: 304–11), the spring of that year represented the best chance for revolution: the war was coming to an end, the authorities' forces were stretched and an accumulation of grievances had built up in the manufacturing areas. But did all this amount to a revolutionary threat? For E. P. Thompson the Luddites displayed a 'tendency' towards becoming a 'quasi-revolutionary movement which continually trembled on the edge of ulterior revolutionary objectives'

(1968: 604). And whilst Thomis and Holt concede that Luddism was well organised and possessed very strong communal solidarity, its aims were essentially limited and industrial (1977: 33). Thus the danger or threat, if there was such, soon passed. As the Luddites generally lacked weapons and the support of national leaders like Cobbett or Cartwright, the 'revolutionary impulse' was short-lived (Dinwiddy 1986: 22). Certainly, key members of the authorities appeared untroubled in 1812. Both General Maitland, the commander of the Northern District, and Earl Fitzwilliam, lord lieutenant of Yorkshire, in contrast to some local nervy magistrates, believed the troubles were containable.

Some of the weaknesses, lack of leadership and a lack of a revolutionary vision and ideology were evident in the post-war revolutionary crises, not least the Pentrich Uprising of 1817. This episode, however, did confirm the existence, albeit small, of a revolutionary underground tradition personified in Thomas Bacon, a framework knitter and radical delegate who travelled extensively between London and the North. The talk of insurrection and revolution which was widespread throughout the North at this time had not been initiated by Oliver the Spy. Moreover, it could be argued that the government, with its repressive legislation and over-reaction to such episodes as the March of the Blanketeers, both contributed significantly to popular disenchantment and forced moderate reformers underground. The rising itself was a sorry affair, involving at most a couple of hundred quite reluctant men. But it has been remembered as 'one of the first attempts in history to mount a wholly proletarian insurrection, without any middle-class support' (E. P. Thompson 1968: 733).

By the time of the 1830s Reform Crisis this alliance between middle- and working-class reformers was precisely what made those years the most revolutionary of the period. In his 'social tension' chart, Rostow found that 1832 was the high point (1948: 124). The crisis of 1830–2 comprised four distinct movements, namely Captain Swing in rural areas, the burgeoning trade union movement (not least Doherty's), Irish rebellion and the movement for parliamentary reform; and all these can be placed in the context of successful though limited revolutions in France and Belgium (Rudé 1988: 150). All these movements remained largely separate and, as a consequence, weakened the revolutionary potential of the situation. How close Britain came to revolution in the autumn of 1831 and the 1832 'Days of May' will always remain one of history's unanswerable questions. Unlike previous revolutionary moments the Reform Crisis witnessed a national and well-organised movement incorporating the middle and working classes in mass mobilisation. The ruling class, for its part, was in disarray, without actually having lost its capacity to rule. The other novel element contained within this crisis, when compared with earlier revolutionary phases, was the very openness of the threat of revolt or the 'tactic of coercion' (Thomis and Holt 1977: 85). But historians have wondered how far the middle classes would have been prepared to go. It is unlikely, given the experience of the riots in Nottingham and more especially Bristol, that they would have been prepared to unleash their working-class supporters, since revolution would have quickly developed beyond their control. At bottom, middle-class reformers, who desired only limited parliamentary reform, were as fearful of revolution as was any die-hard Conservative for, as E. P. Thompson observed, they 'carried in their knapsacks a special constable's baton' (1968: 891). For the middle classes, reform was the best insurance against revolution (Tilly 1995: 337), at least until the end of the decade when limited Chartist rebellions broke out.

Whilst the period experienced enormous structural changes to society and the economy, no revolution occurred. Certainly, as we have seen, a number of revolutionary situations and murmurs came and went, but none threatened to convulse society. Most disturbances, mass meetings and 'contentious gatherings' were limited in time, location and objectives and the participants frequently displayed restraint and discipline, as indeed did the leadership. Therefore it has been argued that the crowd 'tamed itself' (Stevenson 1992: 330), and that no one of political importance wanted revolution (Rudé 1988: 158). But this is not to say that British politics was not deeply affected by the experiences of these years. As Tilly concludes, Chartism inherited a vast store of experience, tactics and demands which gave it its mass national dimension (1995: 339).

8
Conclusion

Edward Thompson's influence on this field and period of history has been immense, and his intellectual presence is likely to remain even after his death in 1994. His *Customs in Common* (1991) undoubtedly belongs to that energetic and burgeoning field of eighteenth-century studies investigating enclosure, customs and crime. The 'moral economy' continues to fascinate academic interest so much that the concept has taken on a life and a direction unimagined by its originator (E. P. Thompson 1971). The research of Randall and Charlesworth (2000), for example, is taking the moral economy concept far beyond the food market, as indeed has Scott who has, in *Weapons of the Weak* (1985), brought to the study of South East Asian peasants a new sophistication that might usefully be imported to eighteenth-century England.

The study of rural protest has shown itself to be remarkably vigorous and innovative in other directions, not least the unresolved Wells–Charlesworth argument which debated the relationship between proletarianisation and forms of protest. Further work is perhaps required on protest during the Napoleonic war years and the influence or otherwise of paternalism on social relations and resistance. This debate has until now been located in the narrow confines of East Anglia, Sussex and Kent, yet it is apparent that there still remain counties awaiting some kind of preliminary investigation. Even the heavily researched regions and themes would repay further reinterpretation and review. Captain Swing falls into this category, since the extent and complexity of these riots have been underestimated by Hobsbawm and Rudé (1973). The rediscovery of the English peasant and the impact of enclosure, which Neeson's (1993) and Reed's (1984) work has brought to light, will probably lead to further studies. Slow to bear fruit have been the 'and now to Lower Hardres' (the first village to break threshing machines in 1830) micro-study village community investigations as suggested by Cobb in his review of Hobsbawm and Rudé's *Captain Swing* (Cobb 1969). Reay's work on Hernhill (1990) and most recently Wells's return to Burwash (1997) bring out the rewards that a close examination of communities can achieve. Similarly, the discipline has achieved only a rudimentary level of enquiry when it has come to understanding popular custom and ceremony which Bushaway's pioneering work (1982a) initially brought out.

Such studies of ceremony could usefully be developed in the urban context alongside research which Epstein's excellent essay on symbols encapsulated (1989). In some ways the influence of post-modernism, as expounded by Joyce (1994) and Vernon (1993), may well creep in, especially as the narratives of popular protest, collective action and mass movements are so well known. But historians should guard against complacency. Such well-known and well-researched events as the Gordon Riots still bear new insights, as Sherwood's recent short article on the involvement of black people in the disturbances reveals (1997). In this particular example, the research has revealed something of the relationship of 'some' whites to blacks. Much also still remains to be done on the language of protest. Only one essay, predictably by E. P. Thompson (1975a), exists on threatening and anonymous letters. These letters provide a rich vein of material and an oral link with the working communities of the past. New approaches to old themes such as factory reform could well prove stimulating and provide a much needed boost to this branch of social history. Two areas in particular could provide the 'new blood': women's history and the history of crime, policing and the criminal justice system. In what has been a male-dominated area, focus upon women's involvement and role in protest has been shamefully neglected. Thomis and Grimmett's work (1982) did not significantly progress our understanding of women's contribution, and Bohstedt's essay (1988) on their involvement in food riots has been heavily criticised, not least by E. P. Thompson (1991: 305–36). More influential and significant work has been undertaken on the later period covering the Chartist and Owenite movements (B. Taylor 1983) and, if sources allow, the spotlight should be brought to bear on the earlier years. Alexander, in an important and pioneering article (1984), has emphasised both the masculinity of radical artisan rhetoric and vocabulary of the 1820s and 1830s, and the role men played in the community when negotiating with the authorities, even though women were active in many of the movements. So gender-based have the previous histories been that it has been suggested that the work of Thompson should be retitled 'the making of the male working class' (Vernon 1993: 4), a point of view largely accepted by Clark (1995) who has attempted to place gender back into the analysis of class.

Interest in the history of crime has largely arisen out of the so-called Warwick School which struck out in different directions in the 1970s. Crime and protest might usefully be brought together again in order to examine the nature of the relationship between periods of social tension and more general criminal behaviour. Some of the sources used in the study of the latter might add detail to the former, such as the Pardon Papers in the Public Record Office which until Gatrell's study (1994) had been overlooked by most historians. Perhaps a reinvestigation of the Luddite regions from a crime perspective may also be productive. More generally, historians of social protest and unrest have not fully utilised surviving legal records either at the Public Record Office or in the local archives. Studies which cover long time periods would also, no doubt, throw light on gender issues, especially as women, as is now argued (Feeley and Little 1991), were prosecuted with declining frequency in the nineteenth century.

During this period of enormous economic, political and social change, popular protest displayed, as we have seen, a complex variety of forms which ranged from the food riot to organised trade unions and from Luddism to Chartism. Historians, under the initial inspiration of Hobsbawm, Rudé and Thompson, have spent the past four decades working to understand these manifestations of popular struggle. Where the concepts of class and class conflict were central to earlier explanation, more recent histories have attempted to develop new avenues that incorporate gender, cultural and criminal justice histories. In this process, popular protest has continued to remain an important branch of social history.

Bibliography

This bibliography is intended to provide an introduction to the very extensive literature on themes covered by this text; it is by no means definitive.

Alexander, S. 1984, 'Women, Class and Sexual Difference in the 1830s and the 1840s: Some Reflections on the Writing of a Feminist History', *History Workshop Journal*, 17, 125–49.

Archer, J. E. 1990, *'By a Flash and a Scare': Arson, Animal Maiming and Poaching in Norfolk and Suffolk 1815–1870* (Oxford). Examines covert protest crime and finds it endemic for much of the period.

1997, 'The Nineteenth-Century Allotment: Half an Acre and a Row', *Economic History Review*, 50, 21–36. Allotments are seen as both a cause and a consequence of social tensions.

Babington, A. 1990, *Military Intervention in Britain* (London). A general and conservative account of military action from 1780 to the present day.

Baer, M. 1992, *Theatre and Disorder in Late Georgian London* (London).

Bamford, S. 1967 edn, *Passages in the Life of a Radical* (London). Originally published in 1844.

Baxter, J. L. and Donnelly, F. K. 1974, 'The Revolutionary "Underground" in the West Riding: Myth or Reality?', *Past and Present*, 64, 124–52.

Behagg, C. 1979, 'Custom, Class and Change: The Trade Societies of Birmingham', *Social History*, 4, 455–80.

Belchem, J. 1981, 'Republicanism, Popular Constitutionalism and the Radical Platform in Early Nineteenth-Century England', *Social History*, 6, 1–32.

1985, *'Orator' Hunt: Henry Hunt and English Working-Class Radicalism* (Oxford). The best study of the leading radical.

1991, *Industrialization and the Working Class: The English Experience 1750–1900* (Aldershot). A good general introduction.

1996, *Popular Radicalism in Nineteenth-Century Britain* (Basingstoke). An up-to-date clear guide.

Bohstedt, J. 1983, *Riots and Community Politics in England and Wales 1790–1810* (Cambridge, Mass.). An ingenious study of three contrasting communities, the characteristics of which, in his opinion, largely define the types of popular protest experienced by them.

1988, 'Gender, Household and Community Politics: Women in English Riots 1790–1810', *Past and Present*, 120, 88–122. Emphasis on women in food riots, but one of its flaws relates to the issue of identifying who was in the crowd.

1992, 'The Moral Economy and the Discipline of Historical Context', *Journal of Social History*, Winter, 265–84.

Booth, A. 1977, 'Food Riots in the North West of England 1790–1801', *Past and Present*, 77, 84–107. Excellent regional study during these years of crisis.

1983, 'Popular Loyalism and Public Violence in the North-West of England, 1790–1800', *Social History*, 8, 295–313. An interesting study of the under-researched 'Church and King' mobs, which updates Rudé.

1986, 'The United Englishmen and Radical Politics in the Industrial North West of England, 1795–1803', *International Review of Social History*, 31, 271–97. A close examination of the revolutionary tradition.

Brewer, J. and Styles, J. (eds.) 1983, *An Ungovernable People* (London). Collection of six essays on seventeenth- and eighteenth-century disorders; also contains excellent introduction.

Brock, M. 1973, *The Great Reform Act* (London). One of the standard accounts.

Brown, R. 1998, *Chartism* (Cambridge). Provides a good introduction to the subject.

Bushaway, B. 1981, 'Grovely: Custom, Crime and Conflict in the English Woodland', *History Today*, May, 37–43.

1982a, *By Rite: Custom, Ceremony and Community 1700–1880* (London). Innovative study.

1982b, 'From Custom to Crime: Wood Gathering in Eighteenth- and Nineteenth-Century England: A Focus for Conflict in Hampshire, Wiltshire and the South', in Rule 1982, 65–101.

Bythell, D. 1969, *Handloom Weavers* (Cambridge). Detailed study that updates the Hammonds.

Cannon, J. 1973, *Parliamentary Reform 1640–1832* (Cambridge). See final chapters.

Chambers, J. D. and Mingay, G. E., 1966, *The Agricultural Revolution 1750–1880* (London).

Charlesworth, A. 1979, *Social Protest in a Rural Society: The Spatial Diffusion of the Captain Swing Disturbances of 1830–1831* (Norwich). Historical Geography Research Series, 1.

1983, *An Atlas of Rural Protest in Britain 1548–1900* (London). Contains good maps of all the main rural riots, including food riots, which are accompanied by useful short essays.

1993, 'From the Moral Economy of Devon to the Political Economy of Manchester 1790–1812', *Social History*, 18, 2, 205–17. Critique of Bohstedt.

Charlesworth, A., Gilbert, D., Randall, A., Southall, H. and Wrigley, C. 1996, *An Atlas of Industrial Protest in Britain 1750–1900* (Basingstoke). Format similar to Charlesworth 1983.

Christie, I. 1984, *Stress and Stability in Eighteenth-Century Britain: Reflections on the British Avoidance of Revolution* (Oxford).

Church, R. and Chapman, S. D. 1967, 'Gravener Henson and the Making of the English Working Class', in Jones, E. L. and Mingay, G. E. (eds.), *Land, Labour and Population in the Industrial Revolution* (London), 131–61. Detailed critique of Thompson's Luddism thesis.

Clark, A. 1995, *The Struggle for the Breeches: Gender and the Making of the British Working Class* (London). Pioneering and innovative study.

Cobb, R. 1969, 'A Very English Rising', *Times Literary Supplement*, 11 September.

Colhoun, C. 1982, *The Question of Class Struggle: Social Foundations of Popular Radicalism in the Industrial Revolution* (Oxford).

Darvall, F. 1936, *Popular Disturbances and Public Order in Regency England* (London).

1969, *Popular Disturbances and Public Order in Regency England* (Oxford, 2nd edn). A reprint of Darvall 1936, one of the classic early texts, which concentrates mainly on Luddism.

De Castro, J. P. 1926, *The Gordon Riots* (Oxford). A detailed narrative of the capital's worst riots.

Dickinson, H. T. 1985, *British Radicalism and the French Revolution 1789–1815* (Oxford). A good Historical Association pamphlet.

Digby, A. 1978, *Pauper Palaces* (London). The New Poor Law in Norfolk.

Dinwiddy, J. R. 1974, 'The "Black Lamp" in Yorkshire 1801–1802', *Past and Present*, 64, 113–23. Highly critical of Thompson's use of evidence.

1979, 'Luddism and Politics in the Northern Counties', *Social History*, 4, 33–63.

1980, 'Sir Francis Burdett and Burdettite Radicalism', *History*, 65, 17–31.

1986, *From Luddism to the First Reform Bill* (Oxford). A good Historical Association pamphlet.

1992, *Radicalism and Reform: Britain 1780–1850* (London).

Dobson, C. R. 1980, *Masters and Journeymen: A Pre-history of Industrial Relations 1717–1800* (London).

Donajgrodzki, A. P. (ed.) 1977, *Social Control in Nineteenth-Century Britain* (London). Important collection of essays on social control.

Donnelly, F. K. and Baxter, J. L. 1975, 'Sheffield and the English Revolutionary Tradition, 1791–1820', *International Review of Social History*, 20, 398–423.

Dunbabin, J. (ed.) 1974, *Rural Discontent in Nineteenth-Century Britain* (London).

Dunkley, P. 1979, 'Paternalism, the Magistracy and Poor Relief in England, 1795–1834', *International Review of Social History*, 24, 371–96. Examines the relationship between rural protest and the breakdown in paternalism.

Dyke, I. 1992, *William Cobbett and Rural Popular Culture* (Cambridge).

Eastwood, D. 1994, *Governing Rural England 1780–1840* (Oxford). Useful chapters on policing and order.

1996, 'Communities, Protest and Police in Early Nineteenth-Century Oxfordshire: The Enclosure of Otmoor Reconsidered', *Agricultural History Review*, 44, 35–46.

Edsall, N. 1971, *The Anti-Poor Law Movement 1833–1844* (Manchester). The first detailed narrative account of the resistance offered to the introduction of the New Poor Law.

Elliot, M. 1977, 'The "Despard Conspiracy" Reconsidered', *Past and Present*, 75, 46–61.

Emsley, C. 1979, *British Society and the French Wars 1793–1815* (London).

1983, 'The Military and Popular Disorder 1790–1801', *Society for Army Historical Research*, 61, 10–21. Contains useful detail.

1985a, 'Repression, "Terror" and the Rule of Law in England During the Decade of the French Revolution', *English Historical Review*, 100, 801–25. Good study of Pitt's so-called reign of terror.

1985b, 'The Thump of Wood on a Swede Turnip: Police Violence in Nineteenth-Century England', *Criminal Justice History*, 6, 125–49. Describes the differences between the army and the men in blue.

1991, *The English Police: A Political and Social History* (Hemel Hempstead). The best history of the police.

Epstein, J. 1989, 'Understanding the Cap of Liberty: Symbolic Practice and Social Conflict in Early Nineteenth-Century England', *Past and Present*, 122, 75–118. Excellent study of radical symbols.

Evans, E. J. 1976, *'The Contentious Tithe': The Tithe Problem and English Agriculture 1750–1850* (London). Major study of tensions and the tithe.

Feeley, M. M. and Little, D. L. 1991, 'The Vanishing Female: The Decline of Women in the Criminal Process, 1687–1912', *Law and Society*, 25, 719–57.

Foster, J. 1974, *Class Struggle and the Industrial Revolution: Early Industrial Capitalism in Three English Towns* (London). A marxist analysis.

Gatrell, V. A. C. 1990, 'Crime, Authority and the Policeman State', in Thompson, F. M. L. (ed.), *Cambridge Social History of Britain 1750– 1950*, vol. III (Cambridge), 243–310.

1994, *The Hanging Tree: Execution and the English People 1770–1868* (Oxford).

Geary, D. 1981, *European Labour Protest 1848–1939* (London).

George, D. 1927, 'The Combination Laws Reconsidered', *Economic Journal, Economic History Supplement*, 2, 214–18.

Gilmour, I. 1992, *Riot, Rising and Revolution* (London). A surprisingly sympathetic study of popular protest from the former Tory cabinet minister.

Glen, R. 1984, *Urban Workers in the Early Industrial Revolution* (London).

Gray, R. 1996, *The Factory Question and Industrial England 1830–1860* (Cambridge).

Hamburger, J. 1963, *James Mill and the Art of Revolution* (New Haven). Still useful for the Reform Crisis.

Hammond, J. L. and Hammond, B. 1920, *The Village Labourer 1760–1832* (London). The early classic on rural society, originally published in 1911. Coverage of Swing is geographically limited but their powerful prose has stood the test of time.

1979, *The Skilled Labourer 1760–1832* (London, new edn). Originally published in 1919, this is probably the most highly regarded in their trilogy. Especially useful on Luddism both in the text and in Rule's introduction, which reviews the debates.

Harrison, M. 1988, *Crowds in History: Mass Phenomena in English Towns, 1790–1835* (Cambridge).

Hay, D. 1975, 'Property, Authority and the Criminal Law', in Hay *et al.* 1975, 17–63. Seminal article.

Hay, D., Linebaugh, P., Thompson, E. P. *et al.* 1975, *Albion's Fatal Tree* (London). A good collection of essays from the Warwick School of Social History.

Hayter, T. 1978, *The Army and the Crowd in Mid-Georgian England* (London). The standard work on crowd control in the eighteenth century.

Hibbert, C. 1958, *King Mob* (London). A popular account of the Gordon Riots.

Hobsbawm, E. J. 1968, *Labouring Men* (London). Collection of essays by one of the modern pioneers of popular protest studies. Most important is the original and still useful 'Machine Breakers'.

Hobsbawm, E. J. and Rudé, G. 1973, *Captain Swing* (Harmondsworth). A fine study of the 1830 riots in Southern England which updates the Hammonds' account but should not be treated as definitive.

Holton, R. J. 1978, 'The Crowd in History: Some Problems of Theory and Method', *Social History*, 3, 219–33. Critical of Rudé.

Hone, J. A. 1977, 'Radicalism in London, 1796–1802', in Stevenson 1977a, 79–101.
   1982, *For the Cause of Truth: Radicalism in London 1796–1821* (Oxford).
Hopkins, H. 1985, *The Long Affray: The Poaching Wars in Britain* (London).
Jones, D. J. V. 1982, *Crime, Protest, Community and Police in Nineteenth-Century Britain* (London). Good essays on poaching and arson.
   1989, *Rebecca's Children: A Study of Rural Society, Crime and Protest* (Oxford). Detailed account of the mythical Rebecca.
Joyce, P. 1994, *Democratic Subjects: The Self and the Social in Nineteenth-Century England* (Cambridge). Leading post-modernist account.
King, P. 1984, 'Decision Makers and Decision-Making in the English Criminal Law, 1750–1800', *Historical Journal*, 27, 25–58. Important study which should be read after Hay's essay.
   1989, 'Gleaners, Farmers and the Failure of Legal Sanctions in England 1750–1850', *Past and Present*, 125, 116–50. First detailed study of gleaning.
Kirby, R. G. and Musson, A. E. 1975, *The Voice of the People. John Doherty 1798–1854: Trade Unionist, Radical and Factory Reformer* (Manchester). Title says it all.
Kirk, N. 1989, 'Commonsense, Commitment and Objectivity: Themes in the Recent Historiography of Peterloo', *Manchester Region History Review: Peterloo Massacre Special Issue*, 3, 61–6. Critical of Walmsley and Read.
Knott, J. 1986, *Popular Opposition to the 1834 Poor Law* (London). The most recent study without being the most original. Contains some new insights.
Langbein, J. 1983, 'Albion's Fatal Flaws', *Past and Present*, 98, 96–120. At times bad-tempered.
Laybourn, K. 1992, *A History of British Trade Unionism c. 1770–1990* (Stroud). Useful overview.
Malcolmson, R. W. 1983, '"A Set of Ungovernable People": The Kingswood Colliers in the Eighteenth Century', in Brewer and Styles 1983, 85–127.
Mather, F. C. 1959, *Public Order in the Age of the Chartists* (Manchester). The first study of order. Contains some useful appendices on sizes of early police forces.
Miller, W. 1977, *Cops and Bobbies: Police Authority in New York and London 1830–1870* (Chicago).
Mingay, G. E. (ed.) 1989, *The Unquiet Countryside* (London). New and old essays on rural protest; some originally appeared in Mingay (ed.), 1981, *Victorian Countryside*, 2 vols. (London).
Mitchell, B. and Deane, P. 1971, *Abstract of British Historical Statistics* (Cambridge).

Morris, R. J. 1979, *Class and Class Consciousness in the Industrial Revolution 1780–1850* (London).

Munger, F. 1981, 'Suppression of Popular Gatherings in England, 1800–1830', *American Journal of Legal History*, 25, 111–40. Examines why some riots were repressed in the North West and why others were not. Size matters.

Muskett, P. 1984, 'The East Anglian Riots of 1822', *Agricultural History Review*, 32, 1–13.

Musson, A. E. 1972, *British Trade Unions 1800–1875* (London). Early pamphlet that covers part of the period.

Neal, F. 1988, *Sectarian Violence: The Liverpool Experience 1819–1914* (Manchester).

Neeson, J. 1993, *Commoners, Common Right, Enclosure and Social Change in England 1700–1820* (Cambridge). The most important book to appear on rural society in recent years, as it puts enclosure and the peasant back on the agenda. It also brings to light protest against enclosure.

Oddy, D. J. 1983, 'Urban Famine in Nineteenth-Century Britain: The Effects of the Lancashire Cotton Famine on Working-Class Diet and Health', *Economic History Review*, 36, 67–86.

Orth, J. V. 1991, *Combination and Conspiracy: A Legal History of Trade Unionism 1721–1906* (Oxford). Detailed and technical but definitive on the Combination Acts.

Outhwaite, R. B. 1990, *Dearth, Public Policy and Social Disturbance in England 1530–1800* (Basingstoke). A very useful survey from the Studies in Economic and Social History Series on food rioting, which covers the period up to the 1780s.

Paley, R. 1989, '"An Imperfect, Inadequate and Wretched System"?: Policing London Before Peel', *Criminal Justice History*, 10, 95–130. An excellent and important article.

Palmer, S. 1988, *Police and Protest in England and Ireland 1750–1850* (Cambridge). Enormous volume which examines public order and protest in a manageable and chronological fashion.

Parssinen, T. M. 1972, 'The Revolutionary Party in London', *Bulletin of the Institute of Historical Research*, 45, 266–82.

Peacock, A. 1965, *Bread or Blood: A Study of Agrarian Riots in East Anglia 1816* (London). A good, readable and detailed study of the 1816 riots.

    1974, 'Village Radicalism in East Anglia, 1800–1850', in Dunbabin 1974, 27–61. Covers a wide spectrum of rural protest crimes.

Peel, F. 1968 edn, *The Rising of the Luddites, Chartists and Plug-Drawers* (London). An oral link with the disturbances, originally published in 1880.

Philips, D. 1980, 'A New Engine of Power and Authority: The Institutionalisation of Law and Enforcement in England 1780–1830', in Gatrell, V., Lenman, B. and Parker, G. (eds.), *Crime and the Law: The Social History of Crime in Western Europe Since 1500* (London), 155–89.

Prothero, I. 1979, *Artisans and Politics in Early Nineteenth-Century* (London).

Radzinowicz, L. 1968, *A History of English Criminal Law and Its Administration*, vol. IV, *Grappling for Control* (London). Detailed account of policing protest.

Randall, A. J. 1982, 'The Shearmen and the Wiltshire Outrages of 1802: Trade Unionism and Industrial Violence', *Social History*, 7, 283–304.

1988, 'The Industrial Moral Economy of the Gloucestershire Weavers in the Eighteenth Century', in Rule 1988, 29–51.

1991, *Before the Luddites* (Cambridge). Excellent study of the South West woollen industrial community and its propensity to protest in the years before Luddism.

Randall, A. and Charlesworth, A. (eds.) 1996, *Markets, Market Culture and Popular Protest in Eighteenth-Century Britain and Ireland* (Liverpool).

(eds.) 2000, *Moral Economy and Popular Protest: Crowds, Conflict and Authority* (London). Nine essays which examine the latest thoughts on the moral economy.

Randall, A. and Newman, E. 1995, 'Protest, Proletarians and Paternalists: Social Conflict in Rural Wiltshire 1830–1850', *Rural History*, 2, 205–27.

Read, D. 1958, *Peterloo: The 'Massacre' and Its Background* (Manchester). Still one of the best accounts of the 'massacre'.

Reaney, B. 1970, *The Class Struggle in Nineteenth-Century Oxfordshire* (Oxford). A useful History Workshop pamphlet from Ruskin College, Oxford.

Reay, B. 1990, *The Last Rising of the Agricultural Labourers* (Oxford). New look at the bizarre Bosenden Wood episode. Especially interesting for the research methodology.

Reed, M. 1984, 'The Peasantry of Nineteenth-Century England: A Neglected Class?', *History Workshop*, 18. Makes a case for resurrecting the English peasantry.

Reed, M. and Wells, R. (eds.) 1990, *Class, Conflict and Protest in the English Countryside 1700–1880* (London). Contains all the articles from the *Journal of Peasant Studies* on the lively Wells–Charlesworth debate, plus new chapters from the editors.

Richardson, R. 1987, *Death, Dissection and the Destitute* (London). Fascinating; includes detail of riots against the Anatomy Act.

Richardson, T. L. 1993, 'Agricultural Labourers' Standard of Living in Lincolnshire 1790–1840: Social Protest and Public Order', *Agricultural History Review*, 4, 1–18.

Rogers, N. 1988, 'The Gordon Riots Revisited', *Canadian Historical Association Historical Papers*, 16–34. Reviews earlier interpretations and attempts to modify Rudé's account by arguing that the mob's anger was directed at customary targets in addition to the gaols and Catholic property.

Rogers, P. G. 1961, *Battle in Bosenden Wood* (Oxford). The original study.

Rose, M. E. 1966, 'The Anti-Poor Law Movement in the North of England', *Northern History*, 1, 70–91. A pioneering study by the recognised authority.

Rose, R. B. 1960, 'The Priestley Riots of 1791', *Past and Present*, 18, 66–88. The original work on the unfashionable loyalist mobs to which all subsequent studies refer.

Rostow, W. W. 1948, *The British Economy of the Nineteenth Century* (Oxford). The social tension chart is still referred to.

Rowe, D. J. 1977, 'London Radicalism in the Era of the Great Reform Bill', in Stevenson 1977a, 149–76.

Royle, E. 1996, *Chartism* (London). The latest edition has been updated.

Rudé, G. 1964, *The Crowd in History* (New York). One of the pioneering masterpieces which helped establish renewed interest in popular protest.

1973, 'Protest and Punishment in Nineteenth-Century Britain', *Albion*, 5, 1–23. A shorter version of Rudé 1978.

1974, 'The Gordon Riots: A Study of the Rioters and Their Victims', in Rudé, *Paris and London in the Eighteenth Century* (London), 268–92.

1978, *Protest and Punishment* (Oxford). A study of social protesters transported to Australia.

1988, 'Why Was There No Revolution in England in 1830 or 1848?', in Kaye, H. (ed.), *Selected Essays of George Rudé: The Face of the Crowd* (Atlantic Highlands, N.J.), 148–63. Useful anthology of some of Rudé's articles.

Rule, J. 1979, 'Social Crime in the Rural South in the Eighteenth and Nineteenth Centuries', *Southern History*, 1, 135–53. Important essay, now reprinted in Rule and Wells 1997.

1981, *The Experience of Labour in Eighteenth-Century England* (London).

(ed.) 1982, *Outside the Law: Studies in Crime and Order 1650–1850* (Exeter). Good essay on sheep stealing by Rule, reprinted in Rule and Wells 1997, and one by Wells on militia riots in 1795.

1986, *The Labouring Classes in Early Industrial England 1750–1850* (London). A good overview.

(ed.) 1988, *British Trade Unions 1750–1850: The Formative Years*. Excellent essays from recognised authorities.

1992, *Albion's People: English Society 1714–1815* (London). See ch. 8 on social and industrial protest.

Rule, J. and Malcolmson, R. (eds.) 1993, *Protest and Survival. The Historical Experience: Essays for E. P. Thompson* (London). Good chapter by Rule on trade unions.

Rule, J. and Wells, R. 1997, *Crime, Protest and Popular Politics in Southern England 1740–1850*. Essays cover food riots, crime and radicals.

Scott, J. C. 1985, *Weapons of the Weak: Everyday Forms of Peasant Resistance* (New Haven and London). Moral economy in South East Asia.

Shelton, W. J. 1973, *English Hunger and Industrial Disorders* (London). Has been superseded by more recent works.

Sherwood, M. 1997, 'Blacks in the Gordon Riots', *History Today*, December, 24–8.

Silver, A. 1967, 'The Demand for Order in Civil Society', in Bordua, D. (ed.), *The Police: Six Sociological Essays* (New York), 1–24.

Smith, P. T. 1985, *Policing Victorian London* (Westport, Conn.). Useful on London crowds and the Metropolitan police.

Snell, K. D. M. 1987, *Annals of the Labouring Poor: Social Change and Agrarian England 1660–1900* (Cambridge). Excellent on Southern England.

Stevenson, J. 1974, 'Food Riots in England, 1792–1818', in Quinault, R. and Stevenson, J. (eds.), *Popular Protest and Public Order* (London), 33–74.

(ed.) 1977a, *London in the Age of Reform* (Oxford).

1977b, 'Social Control and the Prevention of Riots in England 1789–1829', in Donajgrodzki 1977, 27–50.

1989, 'Bread or Blood', in Mingay 1989, 23–35.

1992, *Popular Disturbances in England 1700–1832* (London). Excellent second edition which is by far the best overview on the subject. Coverage in first edition (1979) stopped in 1870.

Storch, R. D. 1975, 'The Plague of Blue Locusts: Police Reform and Popular Resistance in Northern England 1840–1857', *International Review of Social History*, 20, 61–90. Seminal article on anti-police riots.

1982, 'Popular Festivity and Consumer Protest: Food Price Disturbances in the Southwest and Oxfordshire in 1867', *Albion*, 14, Winter, 211–34.

1989, 'Policing Rural Southern England Before the Police, 1830–1856', in Hay, D. and Snyder, F. (eds.), *Policing and Prosecution in Britain, 1750–1850* (Oxford), 211–66.

Sykes, R. 1980, 'Some Aspects of Working-Class Consciousness in Oldham 1830–1842', *Historical Journal*, 23, 167–79.

Taylor, B. 1983, *Eve and the New Jerusalem: Socialism and Feminism in the Nineteenth Century* (London). Pathbreaking and important.

Taylor, D. 1997, *The New Police in Nineteenth-Century England* (Manchester). An overview which summarises debates.

Thale, M. (ed.) 1983, *The Autobiography of Francis Place* (Cambridge).
Thomis, M. I. 1970, *The Luddites: Machine-Breaking in Regency England* (Newton Abbot). A conservative account opposed to Thompson.
Thomis, M. I. and Grimmett, J. 1982, *Women in Protest 1800–1850* (London). First attempt at examining the role of women.
Thomis, M. I. and Holt, P. 1977, *Threats of Revolution in Britain 1789–1848* (London).
Thompson, E. P. 1968 edn, *The Making of the English Working Class* (Harmondsworth). The classic account and essential reading, originally published in 1963.
1971, 'The Moral Economy of the English Crowd in the Eighteenth Century', *Past and Present*, 50, 76–136. Pathbreaking study of the *mentalité* of food rioters.
1975a, 'The Crime of Anonymity', in Hay *et al.* 1975, 255–344.
1975b, *Whigs and Hunters: The Origin of the Black Act* (London). Although the book is generally concerned with an earlier period, its final chapter is very relevant on the rule of law.
1991, *Customs in Common* (London). Among the excellent chapters on custom etc. is a robust attack on critics of his thesis of the 'moral economy'.
Thompson, F. M. L. 1981, 'Social Control in Victorian England', *Economic History Review*, 34, 2, 189–208. Timely warning about the dangers of overusing the concept.
Thwaites, W. 1996, 'Oxford Food Riots: A Community and Its Markets', in Randall and Charlesworth 1996, 137–62.
Tilly, C. 1969, *Collective Violence in European Perspective* (Washington, D.C.).
1995, *Popular Contention in Great Britain 1758–1834* (Cambridge, Mass.). Original; based on massive sample.
Tilly, C., Tilly, L. and Tilly, R. 1975, *The Rebellious Century 1830–1930* (London).
Vernon, J. 1993, *Politics and the People: A Study in English Political Culture c. 1815–1867* (Cambridge). Adopts a new approach.
Vogler, R. 1991, *Reading the Riot Act* (Milton Keynes). A comprehensive history of the act and the relationships between the magistracy, police and the army up to the 1981 riots.
Walmsley, R. 1969, *Peterloo: The Case Re-opened* (Manchester). A blow-by-blow account of the actual day, which fails to place Peterloo in a wider context. Also keen to exonerate magistrates and yeomanry.
Walton, J. K. 1987, *Lancashire: A Social History, 1558–1939* (Manchester). Ch. 8 worth consulting for details of popular radicalism in this important county.
1999, *Chartism* (London). Latest pamphlet on the subject.

Ward, J. T. 1962, *The Factory Movement, 1830–1855* (London). A detailed history of this now little-studied movement.

   (ed.) 1970, *Popular Movements c. 1830–1850* (London). Despite its age, still useful essays on the Factory Movement and anti-Poor Law popular protest.

Wearmouth, R. F. 1945, *Methodism and the Common People of the Eighteenth Century* (London). Dated.

Webb, S. and Webb, B. 1911, *History of Trade Unionism* (London). Originally published 1894.

Wells, R. A. E, 1977, *Dearth and Distress in Yorkshire 1793–1802*, Borthwick Papers, no. 52.

   1978, 'Counting Riots in Eighteenth-Century England', *Bulletin of the Society for the Study of Labour History*, 37, 68–72.

   1983, *Insurrection: The British Experience 1795–1803* (Gloucester).

   1988, *Wretched Faces: Famine in Wartime England 1793–1801* (Gloucester). Erudite and detailed; definitive in its coverage.

   1989, 'British Avoidance of Revolution in the 1790s Revisited', *Bulletin of the Society for the Study of Labour History*, 54, 32–9.

   1994, 'E. P. Thompson, Customs in Common and Moral Economy', *Journal of Peasant Studies*, 21. Useful review of Thompson's most important works.

   1997, 'Mr William Cobbett, Captain Swing and King William IV', *Agricultural History Review*, 45, 34–48. Brings political considerations back into Swing.

White, R. J. 1968, *Waterloo to Peterloo* (Harmondsworth). Popular if slightly dated narrative of a potentially revolutionary period.

Williams, G. A. 1968, *Artisans and Sans-Culottes: Popular Movements in France and Britain During the French Revolution* (London).

Wright, D. G. 1988, *Popular Radicalism: The Working-Class Experience 1780–1880* (London). Useful overview.

Index

New Studies in Economic and Social History

Titles in the series available from Cambridge University Press:

1. M. Anderson, *Approaches to the history of the Western family, 1500–1914*
   ISBN 0 521 55260 5 (hardback) 0 521 55793 3 (paperback)
2. W. Macpherson, *The economic development of Japan, 1868–1941*
   ISBN 0 521 55792 5 (hardback) 0 521 55261 3 (paperback)
3. R. Porter, *Disease, medicine, and society in England: second edition*
   ISBN 0 521 55262 1 (hardback) 0 521 55791 7 (paperback)
4. B. W. E. Alford, *British economic performance since 1945*
   ISBN 0 521 55263 X (hardback) 0 521 55790 9 (paperback)
5. A. Crowther, *Social policy in Britain, 1914–1939*
   ISBN 0 521 55264 8 (hardback) 0 521 55789 5 (paperback)
6. E. Roberts, *Women's work 1840–1940*
   ISBN 0 521 55265 6 (hardback) 0 521 55788 7 (paperback)
7. C. Ó Gráda, *The great Irish famine*
   ISBN 0 521 55266 4 (hardback) 0 521 55787 9 (paperback)
8. R. Rodger, *Housing in urban Britain 1780–1914*
   ISBN 0 521 55267 2 (hardback) 0 521 55786 0 (paperback)
9. P. Slack, *The English poor law 1531–1782*
   ISBN 0 521 55268 0 (hardback) 0 521 55785 2 (paperback)
10. J. L. Anderson, *Explaining long-term economic change*
    ISBN 0 521 55269 9 (hardback) 0 521 55784 4 (paperback)
11. D. Baines, *Emigration from Europe 1815–1930*
    ISBN 0 521 55270 2 (hardback) 0 521 55783 6 (paperback)
12. M. Collins, *Banks and industrial finance 1800–1939*
    ISBN 0 521 55271 0 (hardback) 0 521 55782 8 (paperback)
13. A. Dyer, *Decline and growth in English towns 1400–1640*
    ISBN 0 521 55272 9 (hardback) 0 521 55781 X (paperback)
14. R. B. Outhwaite, *Dearth, public policy and social disturbance in England, 1550–1800*
    ISBN 0 521 55273 7 (hardback) 0 521 55780 1 (paperback)
15. M. Sanderson, *Education, economic change and society in England*
    ISBN 0 521 55274 5 (hardback) 0 521 55779 8 (paperback)

16. R. D. Anderson, *Universities and elites in Britain since 1800*
    ISBN 0 521 55275 3 (hardback) 0 521 55778 X (paperback)

17. C. Heywood, *The development of the French economy,*
    1700–1914
    ISBN 0 521 55276 1 (hardback) 0 521 55777 1 (paperback)

18. R. A. Houston, *The population history of Britain and Ireland*
    1500–1750
    ISBN 0 521 55277 X (hardback) 0 521 55776 3 (paperback)

19. A. J. Reid, *Social classes and social relations in Britain*
    1850–1914
    ISBN 0 521 55278 8 (hardback) 0 521 55775 5 (paperback)

20. R. Woods, *The population of Britain in the nineteenth century*
    ISBN 0 521 55279 6 (hardback) 0 521 55774 7 (paperback)

21. T. C. Barker, *The rise and rise of road transport, 1700–1990*
    ISBN 0 521 55280 X (hardback) 0 521 55773 9 (paperback)

22. J. Harrison, *The Spanish economy*
    ISBN 0 521 55281 8 (hardback) 0 521 55772 0 (paperback)

23. C. Schmitz, *The growth of big business in the United States and*
    Western Europe, 1850–1939
    ISBN 0 521 55282 6 (hardback) 0 521 55771 2 (paperback)

24. R. A. Church, *The rise and decline of the British motor industry*
    ISBN 0 521 55283 4 (hardback) 0 521 55770 4 (paperback)

25. P. Horn, *Children's work and welfare, 1780–1880*
    ISBN 0 521 55284 2 (hardback) 0 521 55769 0 (paperback)

26. R. Perren, *Agriculture in depression, 1870–1940*
    ISBN 0 521 55285 0 (hardback) 0 521 55768 2 (paperback)

27. R. J. Overy, *The Nazi economic recovery 1932–1938: second*
    edition
    ISBN 0 521 55286 9 (hardback) 0 521 55767 4 (paperback)

28. S. Cherry, *Medical services and the hospitals in Britain,*
    1860–1939
    ISBN 0 521 57126 X (hardback) 0 521 55784 5 (paperback)

29. D. Edgerton, *Science, technology and the British industrial*
    'decline', 1870–1970
    ISBN 0 521 57127 8 (hardback) 0 521 57778 0 (paperback)

30. C. A. Whatley, *The Industrial Revolution in Scotland*
    ISBN 0 521 57228 2 (hardback) 0 521 57643 1 (paperback)

31. H. E. Meller, *Towns, plans and society in modern Britain*
    ISBN 0 521 57227 4 (hardback) 0 521 57644 X (paperback)

32. H. Hendrick, *Children, childhood and English society, 1880–1990*
    ISBN 0 521 57253 3 (hardback) 0 521 57624 5 (paperback)

33. N. Tranter, *Sport, economy and society in Britain, 1750–1914*
    ISBN 0 521 57217 7 (hardback) 0 521 57655 5 (paperback)

34. R. W. Davies, *Soviet economic development from Lenin to Khrushchev*
    ISBN 0 521 62260 3 (hardback) 0 521 62742 7 (paperback)

35. H. V. Bowen, *War and British society, 1688–1815*
    ISBN 0 521 57226 6 (hardback) 0 521 57645 8 (paperback)

36. M. M. Smith, *Debating slavery: the antebellum American South*
    ISBN 0 521 57158 8 (hardback) 0 521 57696 2 (paperback)

37. M. Sanderson, *Education and economic decline in Britain, 1870 to the 1990s*
    ISBN 0 521 58170 2 (hardback) 0 521 58842 1 (paperback)

38. V. Berridge, *Health policy, health and society, 1939 to the 1990s*
    ISBN 0 521 57230 4 (hardback) 0 521 57641 5 (paperback)

39. M. E. Mate, *Women in medieval English society*
    ISBN 0 521 58322 5 (hardback) 0 521 58733 6 (paperback)

40. P. J. Richardson, *Economic change in China c. 1800–1950*
    ISBN 0 521 58396 9 (hardback) 0 521 63571 3 (paperback)

41. J. E. Archer, *Social unrest and popular protest in England, 1780–1840*
    ISBN 0 521 57216 9 (hardback) 0 521 57656 3 (paperback)

Previously published as

Studies in Economic and Social History

Titles in the series available from the Macmillan Press Limited

16. J. Thirsk
England's agricultural regions and agrarian history, 1500–1750

17. J. R. Ward
Poverty and progress in the Caribbean, 1800–1960

Economic History Society

The Economic History Society, which numbers around 3,000 members, publishes the *Economic History Review* four times a year (free to members) and holds an annual conference.

Enquiries about membership should be addressed to

The Assistant Secretary
Economic History Society
PO Box 70
Kingswood
Bristol
BS15 5TB

Full-time students may join at special rates.